Path to Truth
The Ray Stanton Story

Ray Stanton

© 2018
© 2022 2nd Edition

ISBN #: 978-1-958792-02-5

Edited by: Mr. Editor
Cover Design by Donna Cook
First Edition © 2016, Updated 2018
Second Edition 2022

Acknowledgements

First and foremost, I acknowledge God for saving my life through His son Jesus Christ. In Christ I have found a Friend indeed. He has changed my very existence and can do the same for you.

I also need to acknowledge my wife Debi, without her help I would never have been able to get this story in print. She is the very example of a Proverbs 31 woman. I thank God every day for her.

Preface

As I sit here reflecting on my life, I'm trying to remember the most interesting parts and hoping that it will make a difference in your life. One thought goes through my mind, "Has it really been that long ago?" The memories come flooding back to me and I think about what a journey it has been.

That's what life is, it is a journey. The most important part is not wealth, it's not success in business, not even homes or property. It is not fame or fortune. The most important things about this journey we call life are the relationships that we develop while living in this flesh.

The first and foremost important relationship is the relationship you have with God. Second, is your relationship with your spouse and your family. Last, comes your relationship with others that you may meet while on your journey. Those relationships are the only real legacy we leave behind. It took me quite a few years to realize this, but today I walk every day with God in my life. I hope this book gives you strength through adversity.

The Beginning

The best place to start is from the beginning. The earliest memories I have are at about two-years-old. Mom and Dad never started their lives together with much and I remember living in a little camper-type trailer parked on the edge of a field. Just across the dirt lane was some woods. It was out in the middle of nowhere, or so it seemed to me. The camper we lived in had no water and no toilet. It was very primitive. I clearly remember the bitter cold winters and the hot, hot summers. It was a new world and everything was exciting.

I remember one nice, spring day Mom was cleaning and let me and my younger brother play outside the trailer. Suddenly, as we were playing, we noticed something in an empty glass gallon-sized cider jug that dad was using to carry water in. It was a sleek little blue tailed lizard he had gotten in the jug and was running around trying to find his way out. I turned the jug over and stuck my finger in the mouth of the jug trying to get that lizard; he would run away, but finally, I managed to turn the jug up so he slid out and when he did I grabbed him. My brother and I were looking at him and playing with him when I heard Mom yell in a loud excited voice, "Put that thing down!"

I was still thinking about what she had just said when she said, in a voice filled with terror, "Give it here". She stretched her hand toward me. So, what did I do? I laid that lizard right in her hand and let go. Well, her voice may have been full of terror before, but this time she let out a blood-curdling scream and threw the lizard. He went sailing one way; she grabbed my brother and I, one in each hand and fled. I had never seen Mom shake like that before, but she shivered and shook. It didn't seem like she would ever stop. I, however, was more concerned with what happened to the lizard.

One of my best memories is when my uncle Don came over one day with a present for us. It was a little Dalmatian puppy; he was an excited little guy and he quickly became a part of the family.

Mom said, "Oooohhh look at this little dog what should

we call him?"

I didn't have a large vocabulary and I said, "deek", so that was it, his name was Deek. Anywhere Kenny and I went, Deek was always with us.

As time went on, we made a new friend. He was an old guy that would come over and take care of an ancient cemetery located in the woods across the lane. He was a nice old guy and he always talked to us kids. We would watch him walking around in the woods. As the summer went on, I began to follow him into the woods to see what exactly he was doing. Later on, when my younger brother Kenny was old enough to start walking, we would both follow him around. He never seemed to mind. Actually, he got a kick out of us exploring the woods. If we got too far away from the trailer, he would see to it that we scooted right back home. Soon, our days were filled with exploring and I must say, it was a good experience. Even as we grew older, we continued to explore the woods. We got braver and braver and would go deeper and deeper into those woods. It was always an adventure for me and Kenny.

Times were always hard for our family. Dad and Mom were trying to raise two boys with very little money. Needless to say, it was a very poor existence, but we made do.

My grandparents would often help us out. Their house was a warm, old place and we felt comfortable there. They had twelve children and my dad was the oldest. Whenever we would go to their house for a visit, it was always an adventure. There were aunts, uncles and cousins there most of the time. The family was always busy and you could feel the love that my grandparents had for their entire family.

My grandma was always cooking and cleaning. Believe me that was a monumental task with so many people around. It seemed that they had the best food; my grandmother was such a great cook. My grandpa and the older boys took care of the livestock. There were cows, hogs, chickens and of course dogs. They did some grain farming and took care of a large apple orchard. It was just the kind of place a group of little boys needed to learn about all sorts of things. My brother and I and our cousins that were around our age had a great time playing together and exploring the farm. The best part was the warmth and love that we felt there.

After about two years of living in the camper trailer, I remember hearing my grandpa tell my dad that he needed to do something more. He explained that we couldn't spend another winter in that trailer. It wasn't safe and it was not warm enough for us to be able to stay there during the harsh winters of Indiana.

My dad seemed really hurt that my grandpa had said something to him about it. He felt he was doing all that he could to get us out of there and into a real home. My grandpa wasn't buying it and I remember they argued a little. I would say, my granddad won that battle. Grandpa told my dad he knew of a small farm with a house that was vacant. It had been empty for a long time, but it had a little land with it. The lady who owned it, Mrs. Opal Parker, was willing to let us farm the land for half the profit and live in the old house.

The Opal Parker Place

A short time later, we were riding along in Dad's car on our way to talk with Mrs. Parker. The meeting went well and Mrs. Parker was a nice old lady who liked little kids. It was great because we liked her and the cookies she gave me and my brother, Kenny, made us like her even more. As Mom and Dad were talking with Mrs. Parker, I heard the adults mention that we were having a little brother or sister. *Hmmm*, I wondered.

After some negotiations, she said we could move into the old place and fix it up however we wanted. As soon as we left her house, with the keys in our hands, we went straight to the old farmhouse. It was back a long lane off the road about a half mile. It was in the middle of farm fields full of corn. We drove back that lane with the weeds grown up in the middle of the lane and it had only a little gravel on the side of that lane. It was an adventure in itself. Our '56 Oldsmobile 88 was hitting bottom as we drove. It was so far that it looked like there was nothing back that lane. Suddenly, we turned the corner and there was an old run down barn on the right side of the lane. A little further back was the old house. The house had an old wooden framed screen door which was hanging off the hinges. It was deserted looking, that was for sure.

Dad stopped the car and Kenny and I couldn't wait to get out. We were so excited. Mom opened the car door and let us out. She warned us not to run off and to stay close. She said, "There may be snakes in the tall overgrown grass of the yard." We were thinking, "*Snakes, Wow! Where are they?*"

I ran around to the side of the house so I could look for the snakes. When I ran around the house, there was this great big thing sitting beside the house. It was metal and went way up in the air. As Dad came up he said, "Hey, we have water on the property. There is the windmill here."

"Windmill, what's a windmill?" I asked.

"Come here, let's see if it works," Dad said.

He messed around pulling this thing and then that thing and all of a sudden something on the top started to spin. It was exciting. At first, it spun very slowly then, it picked up a little speed. All of a sudden, there was a noise and water coming out of a pump at the bottom. My brother and I were in awe.

"Well, no more carrying water in cider jugs, Mom," Dad said.

"Let's go in and see what the house looks like inside," Mom replied.

Dad carefully went up on the rickety-looking wooden front porch to make sure he didn't fall through. Mom was right behind him, with my brother and I following close on their heels. Dad pulled the old screen door open and used the skeleton key to open the rickety front door. The old hinges creaked as the door opened. The door swung open and there before us was a big front room. There was an old wood floor, covered with dust. The floor ran down hill in the middle and then up the other side. The walls had old wallpaper with pieces of the paper hanging here and there. There were cracks in the plaster and it was a hot mess.

As we walked on into the house, it had a room off to the side that was quickly claimed by Mom as her and Dad's bedroom. It was small, but a lot bigger than the camper trailer had been. It had a room straight back through the living room. It was not quite as bad as the living room. The wallpaper was actually not in too bad of condition in this room, but the floor still sagged in the middle.

Next, we looked to the side and there were two steps in the corner going up to a door. Dad said it was the way to the upstairs. He opened the door and started up the stairs with Kenny and me right on his heels.

He stopped and said, "No, stay here."

We reluctantly stopped and scooted back down the stairs. Dad said it was unfinished and the floor needed to be replaced up there. So, Dad closed the door on the stairs and we were not allowed up there.

We then walked straight back toward the rear of the house. We came through another door and there was the kitchen. It actually had a place for a wood stove and a sink along the wall closest to the back door and that big metal thing outside.

"Dad what was that thing again?" I asked.

"What thing?"

"You know, the thing that goes around."

"Oh, that's a windmill."

The next days were full of packing stuff and loading the car with our clothes. We rode with mom taking our things to the new house for one trip after another. My grandpa and grandma came over to see the new *old* house. They said, "Well, it's better than the trailer, but you need some way to heat this old place."

Grandpa and grandma left and in a couple of hours they were back with an old wood stove. Dad and grandpa put it in the kitchen and put up a stove pipe. Grandma had a basket full of food and some curtains to help make it look somewhat better. They left with a promise they would be back the next day.

Just as we were settling down for the night, my grandpa and grandma, my mom's parents, came pulling in from the lane. They had covers and quilts loaded in their car and even more food. They came in and looked around, they said, "We can help fix this place up. We will buy some wallpaper and paste and we can repaper the living room." We were all excited at the possibilities in our new home.

That night we slept on the floor with quilts and covers. We had two kerosene lanterns for light and we had to go out to the outhouse to use the bathroom. But, hey we were boys, so at night we just stepped out the back door and let it go. That's what Dad did, so we boys thought we should, too. At least he would just walk out a little way into the back yard and pee at night. He liked to look up at the stars. I didn't go out as far as he did, but it was still nice to step out the back door and look at the stars. It made me feel like I was growing into a big man.

After a few days, we got the electricity turned on. Finally, we had lights! The lights were on cords that hung from the ceiling. It was nice to be able to see the whole room at night. My grandma and grandpa came over to help repaper the living room. But, the best thing about their visit was they brought me a popgun. It was a rifle style and it made a loud pop. It had a sight on the front of it. I loved it. It was really nice.

Mom and Dad and my grandparents worked all day taking all the old wallpaper off the walls. They filled cracks in the plaster. Then, they put all new wallpaper on the walls. It looked nice, but they didn't put the new wallpaper tight into the corners and it just kind of stuck out from the corner about an inch. To me it just didn't look right. I tried to tell them but they were busy and wouldn't listen to a little four-year-old. So, in order to help them, I took the front sight on my new popgun and poked the sight through the paper in those corners as high as I could reach and tore it all the way to the base boards. Just about the time I had finished the last of the four corners someone noticed how I had *helped*. Oh, they were not happy. I didn't understand why, but they were not happy at all. I was just trying to help.

Life was better as we got settled into that old house. I soon found out that my mom was going to have a baby. She went to the hospital and brought us home a little sister, Darlene. I didn't see what all the fuss was about, but she kept mom busy. Dad would go off to work every day and Kenny and I would play outside and explore.

One day, Dad was mowing the tall grass and brush by hand with a mowing scythe, which is a long hand-held blade. As he cut more and more of the tall grass, a little roof suddenly appeared. When he saw the roof he worked and worked and mowed all around it. There was a little door built into the ground. The roof was unlike anything I had seen. It was down on the ground and in the front was this little door. Dad lifted and tugged and finally got the door to open. There was some steps going down into the ground and then another little door. He went down the steps with me right after him.

"Stay back. Get back!" Dad said as he pried open the other door. There was a little room down there. It had shelves in it.

"What is it, Dad?" I asked.

"It's a root cellar."

"What's a root cellar."

He explained that it was a place to store vegetables and a place to get into if it stormed outside. It may have been all that, but to me it was a place to climb and play and imagine.

One day, my grandpa drove up in his truck. I was excited

to see him. I was even more excited when I saw that he had a couple of pigs in the back. Dad asked him what he was doing with the pigs.

"I'm giving them to you to raise and start your own herd," Grandpa said.

Dad and grandpa started working and made a pen for them in the old barn. Dad gave Kenny and me strict orders to not go around the pigs. They were in the old barn and he said we were not to go in there unless he was with us. When Dad would feed the hogs we would ask to go with him and he didn't mind us tagging along.

Going with Dad to feed the pigs gave us the chance to explore the old barn. There were a lot of old broken or abandoned tools in the barn. As Dad would go through the barn we would ask, "What is that, Dad? What is this, Dad?" He got tired of our endless questions and he would say, "That is a gismo." Of course, I didn't know what a gismo was, but we took Dad at his word. He would sometimes say, "I don't know what that gismo is."

While Dad was at work one day, Kenny and I snuck out to the barn. We were looking around and a huge rat ran out of somewhere and went over by the hogs. It was trapped and snarled at us. I threw a rock at it. Kenny looked for a rock but couldn't find one, but then we saw a piece of an old broken pitchfork. Kenny flung the piece of a pitchfork at it and it was a perfect shot. I don't know how, but it stuck through the rat and killed it. We ran out of the barn and didn't say anything till Dad got home.

When Dad came in, he got a drink of water and headed straight to the barn to feed the pigs. I knew he would see the rat and decided it was better to tell him about what happened before he found out himself.

"Dad, Kenny killed a gismo today."

"A what?"

"Kenny killed a gismo."

He said laughing, "You take me and show me this gismo."

So, out to the barn we went. When he saw the rat, I thought he was having some trouble breathing or something, but he was laughing so hard he could hardly contain himself.

"Boys, that's not a gismo. That's a rat!'

He told the story about the gismo the rest of his life.

The Miscarriage

My mom was pregnant with another baby. We were excited to have another baby brother or sister. Of course, we preferred a brother.

One morning, she was playing with us while Dad was at work. She was picking us up and swinging us around. We were having a great time. She grabbed Kenny and swung him around and all of a sudden she grabbed her stomach. I could see the pain on her face. Suddenly, there was blood everywhere! It was all over the floor. I was afraid.

"Raymond, go get help."

"Where, Mom? Where should I go for help?"

She was in agony, but she said, "Go down to the end of the lane to the closest house. Run Raymond!"

So I ran that long lane as fast as I could and to the nearest house. They had a big dog at that house and I knew he was mean. He was growling and he came at me. He wouldn't let me on their yard. He barked ferociously and growled at me. He ran right up to me as if he was going to attack me. He got right in front of me and I just knew that I was going to be torn to pieces. But, something kept him from jumping on me. He would get right up in my face again and again, but he would always stop. It was the strangest thing.

I was so scared, I didn't know what to do. I ran back up the lane toward home. When I got to the house things were worse, Mom was bleeding badly. She was laying on the bed. I told her what happened.

"Raymond, you have to get help or I will die."

So, I took off down the lane again. This time the dog was even fiercer than he had been before. Still, each time he came at me, he stopped just short of attacking me.

I started yelling and yelling. The dog was growling and snarling. I could tell he wanted to tear into me. No one was coming out of the house, so, finally, I picked up rocks and threw them at the house.

A woman came out of the house.

"What's going on out here?" she asked. I think she could tell by the look on my face that there was trouble.

"Something's wrong with my mom. She needs help. Come quick!"

She put me in her car and we raced back the lane. She rushed in to help mom. She was able to get mom into the car and rushed her to the hospital.

We kids were left there alone. Shortly after they left, the woman's husband rushed back to the house to check on us. He looked me over from head to toe.

"Are you ok? Did my dog bite you?"

"No, I'm fine."

"Son, I don't know why he didn't bite you. He is a guard dog and he bites anyone who comes on our property. He will attack anyone unless we give him the command to stop. You are one brave and lucky young man."

Mom had lost so much blood by the time they arrived at the hospital, they had to give her transfusions. I was worried, but luckily she survived. She'd had a miscarriage and lost the baby. After several days in the hospital, Mom was finally able to come home.

That day stuck in my mind. The one thing I took away from that encounter with the dog was, there was *something* that had stopped that dog. There was *something* that kept him from tearing me apart. *Something* out of my control had stopped him. I just didn't know what.

The Tractor

We made it through that first year in the new house and things seemed to be pretty normal. It was a time for us to explore and find new things. Actually, at this point, everything was new and exciting for us. My brother and I and Deek, of course, would play and challenge each other daily. Seemed we were never short on finding fun and trouble.

We were still farming. One time, after the corn had been picked, Dad decided to glean the fields. What is gleaning you might ask? Well, we would walk along beside the old tractor with a trailer being pulled behind it. We would pick the corn up off the field that the picker had missed and throw it in the trailer. Dad must have gotten frustrated, because we weren't very fast. He told me that he and mom could do it a lot faster if I drove the tractor. So, he told me exactly what to do, then he put the tractor in low gear and let me drive.

All was well until it came time to stop. I couldn't stop it. Dad yelled, "Stop!"

I pushed the clutch in as far as I could, but I couldn't hold it in. I was barely even able to reach the pedal. My foot came off the clutch and the tractor jumped forward. Oops, it went through the fence. I kept trying and I finally got it stopped. I had made a mess of the fence that surrounded the field. Dad was irate. No, he was worse than irate, he blew up! Blew a gasket is what we called it.

Dad yelled and yelled at me. I knew I was in trouble. We were trying to make a little money to buy groceries by gleaning the fields. I had ruined the fence and it would cost more than the corn we could possibly glean from that field would bring in. He jerked me down off the tractor and beat me. I had been spanked before, but this was more than a spanking. He took all his frustration out on me.   It didn't matter that I was too small to be driving the tractor or that I could barely even reach that pedal.

The next day he put me right back on that tractor even though I told him I didn't want to drive it. I was so scared of making a mistake. I was worried about getting another beating. Somehow, I managed to make it through the day without a problem.

I didn't realize it at the time, but my life had just changed that day. I went from a five-year-old boy with no worries, to a full-time helper for my dad. He started to rely on me much more than he should have for a child that age. But, that was farm life.

I did whatever I could, but he always expected more than I gave. When we went to cut wood for the winter, I no longer watched, but it was my job to carry the wood. For the first time in my life I had responsibilities. It was just the way it was.

The winters were cold. We worked all the time trying to get wood in. It was something I would understand later, but Dad hadn't brought in enough wood for the winter before cold weather hit. We were always out in the woods in the worst part of the winter. We were always cold trying to get more wood. He never prepared properly during the warm months for the upcoming winter. I learned at an early age, that it pays to be prepared before the long, cold winter hits in Indiana.

The next summer came and went and I helped out around the farm as much as I could.

The next fall I started school. My uncles, who were twins, were ten years older than me and they had me convinced school was going to be terrible. They were both characters. They got me in all sorts of trouble. Most of the time, I didn't know any better, so I just went along for the ride.

My mom had a talk with my uncle Dan and made him help her to assure me that they were just kidding me. They promised me it wasn't that bad. They were right the first time. I hated school from the very first day. I just didn't fit in.

Mom always told me the truth and after the things my uncles had put me through on a regular basis, I believed Mom instead of them. My first day of school started off ok. Mom had taken me in and introduced me to the teacher and then she left. There we were a bunch of little six-year-olds just looking lost. We were all standing and looking all around and at each other.

I saw another mom bring in this big kid named Wes. He didn't want to be there and when she left, he started crying so loud that it had all of us scared to death. We all started crying. We were thinking, *"If this great big kid was scared, it had to be bad."*

I got through first grade, but it was torture for me to sit in the classroom all day. I was so used to being home and being outside. Recess was the best part of the day, but sitting in that desk all day was absolutely horrible. I kept looking outside, yearning to be out there. It was hard for me to cope with. I made it through that first year, but it wasn't easy.

During that first year and for many more years, I was going to school during the day and working on the farm helping dad with the chores, before and after school. When school was out for the summer, it was a reprieve. Nothing could convince me that school was really necessary. I hated school! I wanted to be home. We worked hard, but it was my life.

One day, I was visiting my grandpa.

"Hey, Grandpa, where are my uncles?" I asked.

"They are out in the pasture."

So, I headed out to the pasture to see them. They were playing army with Daisy BB guns. Just as I got close enough to them, they caught me in the crossfire. I got shot with BB's about ten times, Man did it sting, and I ran out of the pasture and right past Grandpa.

"What's wrong with you, boy?" he asked as I ran by.

"They shot me with BB's," I blurted out through a stream of tears. I was gasping for breath.

Grandpa took off across that field, over to the fence and yelled for them. Man, when they came up out of the field, he chewed them out up one side and down the other. Then, he took their BB guns and bent the barrels over his knee and threw them up into a big overhead water tank. Off came his belt and he spanked them all the way to the house, as they ran kicking and screaming.

I remember another time when they coaxed me into coming over to where they were standing. When I got close, I noticed they were pointing to a girl.

"You see that girl over there?" they asked. Now, bear in mind that they were probably sixteen years old at this point and I was only six.

"Yes," I said.

"Well," they said, "she likes for guys to squeeze her

boobs. Go over and squeeze her boob." They held up their hands making a cupping motion.

"No, no way," I said.

Finally, after they insisted and kept coaxing me until I believed them. They promised me some candy or something, I really don't remember. So, I gingerly walked over and said hi to the young lady. She said hi back and I just reached my hand out and grabbed her right boob. Whew! That was all it took. She let me have it. She hit me so hard I swear I heard bells. I turned around and my uncles were laughing so hard they were rolling on the ground. That's the kind of trouble they got me into most of my young life.

Kenny was old enough now to start helping with chores around the farm now. I liked being out of school for the summer, but it seemed like we kept getting more and more chores added to our already long list. We stayed busy working on the farm all summer, but there was some time for play.

Before I knew it, summer was over and school was starting again. I dreaded it. In the second grade, I had this old lady teacher, Mrs. Boggs. She was firm, but she really loved kids and knew how to deal with each type of student. I wasn't paying attention one day and just kind of doing my own thing.

She called out my name.

"Raymond!"

Oh, no! I thought.

"Come up here, Raymond."

She made me sit on her lap while she taught class. Oh, it was so embarrassing. Boy, she taught me a lesson and she didn't have any more trouble with me. I liked her, though, and she was the best teacher I ever had.

That same year, I found out that we are moving again. It was maybe March or April. I had just started getting used to the school. I had made friends and even had my first girlfriend. I finally had a teacher I really liked. She was the one teacher who knew me and knew how to handle me. Now we are moving again.

Dad had an opportunity to take on a bigger farm way on the other side of the county. We were farming on the halves, which is like sharecropping. This farm was more than five times the acreage.

They had cows and sheep on this farm. Dad felt it was a big step up and the house and barns were much better. So, whether we kids liked it or not, that's the way it was. We were packed up and moved across the county to a new farm and a new place to live, The Kehrt farm.

The Kehrt Farm

The whole family drove over to look at the new farm. It was a long trip, but we finally turned onto a little gravel road. The farm was right ahead of us on that road. I was sort of expecting a big lane, but instead it was just a little road. It was a really nice farm compared to what we currently had and there was a house with gray siding and a little detached garage. There was the outhouse, the chicken coop, a big barn in really good shape compared to the last one, and a corn crib.

I thought, "*Wow! This is really something.*"

"Oh, look across the road. All that land goes with this farm," said Dad.

I looked across the road and there was another big barn for cattle and a large equipment shed on a hill across the road.

When we went in the house and there was a kitchen sink with a real faucet. It even had running water in the house. No more having to fetch water every day. It was amazing to us kids. We excitedly ran all through the house, but, alas, there was no indoor bathroom. We were still going to have to use the outhouse. The outhouse was just out the back door and down the little path behind the garage. At that moment, it didn't really matter. We were excited that we had a big yard and a lot of new adventures awaited.

The Move

The first week of our move into the Kehrt Farm, I was still in school where we were currently living. Every day, Mom would take Dad to work, see me off to the bus, then drive a load of our stuff across the county to our new house. Poor Mom, she would then have to hustle back to the old house to be there when I got off the bus. I'm sure it was a hectic time for her, but I think she was excited to move into the new house with the running water, so it was probably worth it to her.

The New Shoes

I n the middle of our move, Dad noticed that my shoes were practically falling off my feet, so he stopped in town and got me some new lace up farm shoes. There we were in the middle of the move and yet they took the time to get me those shoes. It was pretty exciting. Well, I think it was either that or I went to the new school barefoot. Dad sat me down and made sure that I understood that if those shoes got torn up, I would get the beating of my life.

Two days later, Mom saw me off to school and took off with a load of stuff across the county to the new place. That day, it started to rain and it rained and rained. It was one of the worst floods to hit the area on record; roads were washed out and it was a mess.

When I got off the bus to head down the lane, I saw all these mud puddles. They were everywhere. I could still hear my dad telling me, 'Don't get those shoes wet. You better not be walking through mud puddles in those.' So, I carefully picked my way around the mud puddles until the mud and water were completely blocking the lane even the field was standing water. I looked back and the water was covering the lane all around where I had just come from. I was on the highest ground and it was shrinking rapidly. I knew I was going to be in trouble if I stayed there, but I thought Mom would come looking for me.

When Mom didn't show up, I took my coat off and wrapped it around and over those new shoes to protect them and started yelling for help. What I didn't know was that Mom had gotten stuck on the other side of the county by washed out roads. She wasn't back there and there was no one around to hear me. I stood there for hours. I got so wet and cold. I was shivering so badly. I thought I might die if someone didn't find me soon.

Finally, I saw a car's headlights at the end of the lane. It stopped and then I saw Mom walking and carefully working her way toward me. She was wading through the water. When she reached me she said, "Why didn't you go on to the house and get inside."

"Mom, Dad told me I couldn't get my new shoes wet."

She helped me to the house, got me inside and out of those wet clothes. She covered me up. I was still shivering, so she started rubbing me with the blankets to bring my body temperature up. She started building a fire and once the fire was going, we sat there by it, huddled together. Both of us soaked and tired and cold.

We would end up being there, just her and me for a couple of days, the electricity was out the whole time. My grandfather, my mom's dad, finally came back the lane on a tractor. The tractor was the only thing high enough to get back through the flooded lane.

We rode the tractor back down the lane, sitting on the fenders for what seemed like forever.

We saw a car sitting across a big, flooded place in the road. Grandpa drove the tractor through the water. It was deep, but we made it. Grandma was in the car waiting on us with blankets and some food and some water in a mason jar. When we left that house on that tractor, it was my last trip down that lane for years.

We went to my grandparent's house to stay for a couple of days. When we finally left their house, the water had gone down, but many of the roads were washed out. We had to work our way around the big holes caused by the flood. At one hole we actually got out and looked at it. Dad said it was probably thirty feet deep. The road was completely gone for about a quarter of a mile.

New Farm / New School

I soon started at the new school. It was very different from my old school, but it was ok. I started to make a few friends. For the next many weeks, life was all about school, coming home and working to finish chores. I had to feed livestock, do my chores and work, work and more work. We now had a larger farm to take care of, so Dad needed even more help and I was the oldest, so much of the responsibility fell to me.

One day, when I got home from school, I noticed that Dad was at the house. It was during the day, which was very unusual. At 3:30 in the afternoon he was almost never home. He was standing there waiting for me to get off the bus. As I stepped down off the bus, Dad came up to me and said, "I have some bad news for you." I could tell by his face that it wasn't something I wanted to hear.

"What is it?" I asked.

"Deek got hit by a truck today. He didn't make it."

Kenny and I hadn't looked around, but we now noticed that Deek wasn't there. He always met us when we got home. He would be standing there with his tail wagging. Heck, he even ran and jumped on the bus in the mornings if he could get away with it, just so he could go to school with us.

There had been three or four times we tried to sneak him on with us, but the bus driver had run him off that bus many times. Our bus driver was a lady and she wouldn't even open the bus door when we got home till we were ready to step off the bus. She knew Deek was going try to sneak on the bus to welcome us home.

But, Deek was gone and Dad left it up to me and Kenny to do the right thing and bury our dog. Shovels in hand, we followed Dad out to the field, selected the right spot and put him in the ground. As much as it hurt, it gave us a sense of peace at least knowing we did the best we could for him.

We all shared a few tears and told stories of him running and playing with us. We talked about the adventures we had, about the school bus driver trying to get him out from under the school bus seat and how all the kids were trying to help hide him. They wanted him to come to school with us. It was a rough few days. He was definitely missed. I hated doing the chores when he wasn't there beside us. I think farm kids have a special bond with their dogs. I know we did.

Our days were busy even as a child. It seemed it was work, work, and more work, all the time. Once in a while, we kids would get a few minutes to play while Dad was doing something like driving the farm trucks around or something else that we were too young to help with.

We would build forts out of the hay in the barn lofts. It was so much fun. As we got braver being up high in the barn, we began to make rope swings. We could swing from one side of the barn over the equipment bays to the other side lofts. It was great fun and it kept us out of trouble, well, at least partially.

A Little Down Time on the Farm

One day, we had some down time from our chores and were busy pretending we were in some serious battle with the enemy. We were attacking our enemies, when our little sister, Darlene, came up to tell us mom had some work for us to do. We were so into what we were doing we didn't want to stop having fun yet.

"We will be down in a little while," we said.

"Does mom know you are swinging across the barn like that?" asked Darlene.

"No, she doesn't and you better not tell."

Darlene turned and ran to the house and told mom exactly what my brother, Kenny, and I were doing in the barn. Needless to say, Mom was not happy. I know, now, that she was afraid we would be hurt. So, we were grounded from the barn until Dad got back.

"Oh no! She's gonna tell Dad," we thought.

That, she did. She told Dad when he got to the house and boy, did we get in trouble. He lit into us when he found out about the hay forts.

"Don't you boys know that messing up the hay, keeps me from putting more hay away in the barn? Not only that, but you could get hurt!"

He was really angry. He went on and on. We didn't realize we were doing anything wrong, but we felt awful. We were just having fun. Our fun was over and it was ALL Darlene's fault!

We were so mad at Darlene. So, the next opportunity we got, we took my sister's beloved doll and hung her by her neck over a beam in the barn. Oh, we were smart because we placed it just out of her reach. We were going to teach her!

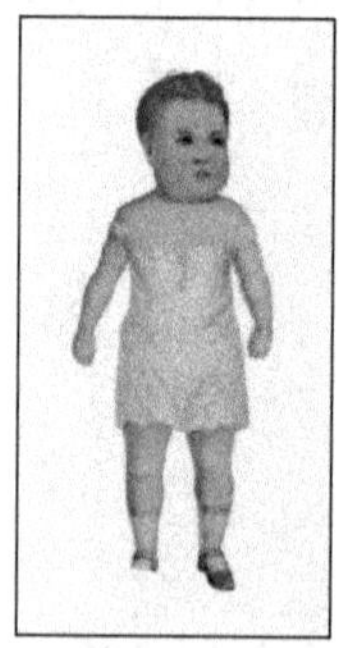

We hid in the loft with the end of the rope in hand and when she came out into the barn, she saw her doll hanging by the neck. She was so upset. She frantically jumped up and reached for it again and again. Every time she reached for the doll, we pulled it up, just out of her reach. We were getting our revenge. Over and over again, she would jump up to try and grab her doll. We would lower it down just close enough to her hands and then pull it back up. We kept it just out of her reach.

Finally, we were laughing so hard, we gave ourselves away and revealed that we were up there in the loft messing with her.

We scowled at her with a warning, "You tell on us again, we will cut this dolls head off and you won't have it anymore." We thought we were so smart.

Now, with another boy, that tactic may have worked, but for little girls we were soon to find out that was the wrong approach. Darlene spun around and ran to the house and once again she told Mom on us. Hey, we had warned her what would happen. Out came the pocketknife and we cut that doll's head right off. Just as we finished, we looked up and there was mom storming up the hill to the barn.

Oh boy, did we get it. Mom didn't spank us often, but this time she broke off a tree limb and she spanked us with a switch. Then, when Dad got home she told him what we had done. Oh, no this wasn't good. We knew we were in for it again. Whew, off came his belt and we got it good, well bad actually, because that spanking was even worse than the one Mom had given us.

We learned that since Darlene was a tattle-tale, we didn't let her know anything that we were doing. She learned a lesson, too, from that day. She learned all she had to do was tell Mom and Dad anything she knew we were doing wrong and we were in trouble. She gained a lot of power over us boys that day. Too much power for a little girl to have.

It was really bad for us because we did lots of things we weren't supposed to be doing. Hey, we were boys! Any time she found out about something we shouldn't be doing, she would tell on us and get us into trouble. Snitch!

Our once little family had grown again. We now had a younger brother, Darrel. Kenny and I were just glad it wasn't another sister. There were four kids and we soon found out mom was expecting again.

With such a large family, it seemed that every time we turned around someone was getting sick. With us three older kids in school, it was just a matter of time before we caught whatever was going around at the time and brought it home to everyone else.

The Measles/Chicken Pox/Mumps

One day, I remember, Kenny came home from school and said he was feeling a little sick. Mom noticed red spots all over him. He looked like a polka dotted kid! He had the three-day measles. So, that meant we all got them.

It took us a while to get over those measles and the next thing we knew, we all came down with the German measles. We were hoping there weren't any more varieties of measles out there. I remember the German measles were really bad. It was so bad, we all had to stay in a dark room for days. We felt miserable, but got through that round of illnesses.

The Chicken Pox came next. Geez, that was even worse than the three-day measles or the German measles. We broke out in blisters all over our body. We had a high fever and when the blisters busted, they became scabs. It was awful. They were everywhere.

Mom told us we were not to scratch them, but it was really hard to resist; they itched so badly. We made it through the Chicken Pox, but it was rough.

Oh my, then came the mumps. What a weird name! I had never heard of anything like it, but it was miserable. We were all in misery. They were under our chins, so our throats swelled and it hurt to even move. Even turning over in our own bed was bad, it hurt to move.

Growing up poor meant in order to use the bathroom, we had an outhouse. Well, when you are sick, you can't go to the outhouse, so we had a chamber pot close by. I remember that even moving to go to the bathroom was torture. We all had to stay in bed for days.

Finally, after what seemed like forever, we started feeling better. We looked outside and the sun was shining through the window, the birds were singing, and we certainly felt fine. So, we asked Mom to let us go outside and play. We were crushed because she said, "No, you have to wait the entire time that the doctor said, or the mumps can go down on you."

Go down on you? What the heck did that mean? When we asked her what she meant she said, "The mumps could go down to your testicles."

Mom left us and headed out to the kitchen to work. Kenny and I had a long talk about those Mumps *going down on us.* We decided we didn't believe it. Mom had never lied to us, but I said, "She's just trying to scare us so we stay in bed,"

Since we knew more than Mom did, we slid the bedroom window up and slid out. We dropped to the ground with a thud. *So far so good.* We snuck out behind the chicken house, so mom couldn't see us and we started playing. We found an old metal barrel. I don't remember which one of us had the bright idea, but the chicken house roof came down at a slope from about ten feet high in the front to about two-feet off the ground in the back, which is where we were.

The plan was to roll the barrel up the roof, climb into the barrel and roll down the rooftop. Sounded fun, right? So, up on the rooftop we went. When we got to the top, Kenny got inside the barrel while I held it. Next, I jumped in and down suddenly, off the roof we went.

We hit the ground with a horrible thud. It felt like my jaws were ripped out. We were both rolling around on the ground in excruciating pain. I can't even explain how badly it hurt. Then, I realized not only did my throat hurt, my groin was hurting, too. Yep, you guessed it, Mom wasn't just trying to scare us, it really happened. The Mumps had *gone down* on us.

This meant we had to lay in bed for another week with ice on our crotch. Oh, the agony and the embarrassment. Sometimes it pays to listen to your mother.

The Skunk

It was fall now and Dad came in one day after we had sold some corn. He excitedly told Mom that we were going to get a Television. We all packed into the car and went to the store and bought a brand new, big black and white television. The store said it was supposed to be portable, but was big, bulky and a very heavy TV. When we finally got that big thing home, Dad was like a little kid with a new toy. He plugged it in right away and turned it on. It took a few minutes for it to warm up, but once it had warmed up, he started flipping channels.

I remember we worked and worked adjusting those rabbit ears and we finally got a show to come in. Funny thing was, it would only come in if someone would hold the antenna a certain way. Well, guess who the *holders of the antenna were?* Yep, you guessed it, Kenny and I got another chore added to our long list. There were no remotes back in those days, so we were now officially the channel turners and the antenna holders.

We started watching a show on that black and white television. I can't remember the name of it, but I do remember there was a kid who had a pet skunk. That skunk was really smart and he seemed to be a good pet. The show was on for just a short while but the impression that *skunks make good pets* was planted in our minds.

That next spring, Dad sent us back into the woods to bring the cattle up to the barn for feeding. It was a beautiful, warm, spring, Saturday afternoon. The sun shining and everything was blooming; it was a great day. We got to explore the woods on our way back to get the cattle. We messed around a little while, then, found the cows and started driving them toward the barn. They were moving steadily on their own but, we lagged back a little.

Suddenly, we saw four little baby skunks crossing the cow path. This was our chance! I raced forward and grabbed one. That little critter scratched and clawed but finally settled down when he realized I wasn't going to hurt him. But, he had sprayed and it was all over both of us. We were so excited at first that we didn't even realize how bad we smelled. We raced up to the barn, skunk in hand, and penned the cows in just as Dad had told us. We ran excitedly over to the house to let the family know we had a new pet. We had caught that skunk ourselves and were so proud. We were just like the kid on TV.

My little sister, Darlene, and brother, Darrel, were on the porch playing and we told them to go get mom. When mom came outside she said, "Oh…. Oh… Oh… NO!! What are you boys doing?" That nasty smell was all everywhere and we still had that little skunk in our hands.

"You get rid of that skunk and then get back up here immediately," she yelled.

We could tell by the tone of her voice there was no sense in arguing. She was mad at us and we really weren't sure why. But, we took the skunk to the edge of the woods and let him go. On the way back to the house we began to realize how bad we smelled and both started throwing up. When we made it to the house, Mom was standing at the door and stopped us both.

"Don't you come too close! Get out of those clothes and take them over to the burn barrel. Burn them!" She threw us some matches.

We were confused. "You want us to burn our clothes?"

"Yes," she said, "Everything but your shoes."

We stood out by the trash barrel naked holding our shoes and lit the clothes on fire. We watched them burn for a few minutes and then headed back up to the house. We had stopped throwing up by now, but we still smelled awful. We were almost to the house where Mom was standing over a #2 wash tub. She was pouring her homemade canned tomato juice into it – lots of it! She made us stay back well away from her. When she was done, she went back onto the porch and told us to get in that tub and wash with tomato juice until the stench went away.

We washed and washed and the stench subsided slightly, but not completely. We thought we were done. We didn't smell as bad as we did. Mom threw us a towel and we dried off. She made us take the tub of nasty smelling tomato juice around behind the chicken house and told us to dump it out.

We headed back up to the house. Mom stepped out of the house, took a big whiff and said, "You two still stink."

We had to fill that wash tub up again with water this time. And, yet, another bath. She held her nose and poured dish washing soap in the tub. We bathed in that tub 'til we were all wrinkly and our skin puckered everywhere. We were finishing up the second bath and Dad came home.

"What is going on here?" he asked.

After Mom told him the story, he came over to where we were. When he smelled us he said, "There is no way you boys are coming in the house tonight. We won't be able to breathe."

So, Kenny and I spent that night and the next on the back porch. They brought us our supper out there and threw some covers out there for us.

Sunday night, Mom made us wash with dish soap one more time. The next day was a school day. When we got on the school bus, our little sister, Darlene lagged behind because she didn't want to be near us smelly boys.

We climbed onto the bus, and the bus driver said, "Oh, my, gosh! You two go sit in the back. You stink!" As we headed to the back of the bus, everyone we passed would hold their nose and say, *PEEEWWW*! Everyone moved toward the front of the bus and away from us. Even our friends moved away. It was not a fun bus ride.

When we got to school, we went to our separate classrooms. My teacher watched as no one wanted to sit close to me and asked what seems to be the problem. Then, she stepped a little closer and I saw the expression on her face change.

"Let's see, Ray lets have you move to the back of the classroom," she said.

I moved to the back and found an empty seat. She tried to make it through class with me stinking something awful, but she only made it for a few minutes.

"I'm sorry, Raymond, but you are going to have to move again."

She had me take my chair out in the hallway. She followed me, at a distance, to the door and shut the door behind me.

So, I was exiled from my class and was sitting out in the hall. After sitting down, I glanced down the hall and there, outside the next classroom, was my brother, Kenny.

"I don't think that we used enough tomato juice do you?" Kenny asked.

"Well, we used all Mom had, so the stink will have to wear off. It will eventually. Remember when Deek got a hold of that skunk? Well, he was ok after a few days. We will just have to be patient."

It took about a week of more serious washing and some notes home from upset teachers before that smell faded. It did teach us a lesson. If you're going to mess with a skunk, even a baby one, make sure you have lots of tomato juice. The bad thing was we had wasted all the tomato juice mom had canned for the winter. That was food out of our mouths.

The Lost Horse

Days pass and then months when you are a kid. We were working and going to school. In our down time, evenings mostly, we watched the TV Dad had bought for the family. Kenny and I had our favorite TV programs; Ponderosa, Cheyenne, Cimarron Strip and Rawhide. At the time, westerns were big and for two farm boys who wanted to be cowboys and live out under the stars, those shows were an inspiration. We longed to hunt for what we needed to eat or to go fishing. But, most of all, we felt we really needed a horse.

As part of our work week, a couple of times a week Kenny and I would have to traipse into the woods to check on the cattle. It was a wonder- filled place back there in the woods. There was a river running through it and it was a great place for two young boys to explore.

One day, we were following a cantankerous old cow who didn't want to leave the woods. She had wandered further back on the property than Kenny or I had ever been before. We finally got her turned around and headed back with the herd. We stumbled upon an old gate that was broken down.

We were checking it out and suddenly, our wildest dream came true. Up walks this great big horse. He was on the other side of the gate. We figured since he was so far back in the woods, he had to be lost. Kenny and I talked to him and he came over to us. *This was great!* We had found some apples earlier on an old tree and had put them in our pockets. We pulled them out and fed them to the horse. Oh, how he loved those apples. We worked and worked together and finally got that broken gate open. We led the horse through the gate and started petting him. We coaxed him over next to a fallen tree and climbed up on his back. We had no idea if this horse had ever even been ridden, but we didn't care. We had a horse!

Away we went; he just loped along and followed the cows up to the barn. We were brave and rode him right up to the front of the house and yelled for mom to come and look.

"Mom, look what we found. Look what we found," we yelled.

Mom came outside and her eyes grew big when she saw both of us on that big old horse. I was in front and Kenny was on the back behind me.

We both yelled at the same time, "Can we keep him? He was lost in the woods and he's tame and he likes us Mom. PLEEEASSE MOM!!! Can we keep him?"

She was flabbergasted and stammered, "What? Where did you find that horse? What on earth!" She finally gained control and said, "Well, tie him to the post out by the chicken house and ask your dad when he comes in."

We anxiously waited for our dad to come up to the house. Dad came into the barn yard; we couldn't contain ourselves any longer. We went screaming out toward him yelling, "Dad, we found a HORSE! He was back in the woods. He was lost and we found him. Can we keep him?"

"What?" he said and spit a wad of chewing tobacco out of his mouth. "What?" he said again.

"We found a horse, Dad. Can we keep him?"

"Where did you find a horse?"

"We found him back in the woods. One of the cows went way back in there and we had to get her out of the woods. We just found this horse. He's tame and he let us ride him and he likes apples."

"Well, where is he? Is he still back there in the woods?"

"No, Dad. We rode him home. He's tied up down at the chicken house."

We were both talking in unison. We had rehearsed every response planned; for every question. That horse was going to be ours. We were sure of it. After all, it was free. Dad couldn't say no to a free horse.

"Well, let's go take a look at this horse you found."

So, we ran ahead and he followed us to the chicken house.

"Where did you find this big old horse again?"

Again, we explained to him about the broken gate we had opened to let the horse come through.

"Oh, I see," he said. "Well, boys this horse looks just like the one our neighbor has over on the other road. His land backs up to ours and now it looks as though you boys have stolen his horse. Do you know what they do to horse thieves?"

Of course! Anyone who watched as many western shows as we did knows what happens to horse thieves. THEY HANG 'EM!!! We were devastated about not getting to keep the lost horse, and now we were gonna be hanged for stealing him. Things couldn't have been worse to two young boys.

"Well, there's only one thing to do. You boys ride that horse over to the neighbors and explain what happened. Hopefully, he will accept your apology. Maybe he will only have you put in jail for a while."

We were scared to death, but we did as Dad said.

We climbed up on that horse and rode him about three miles around to the neighbor's place. Dad was following us in the car. When we rode up, there were a whole bunch of kids playing in the yard. There were some older than us, some our age and some younger than us. There were kids everywhere it seemed.

"Hey, what are you guys doing with our horse?" yelled one of the kids.

Oops, Busted!

We started to explain to them that we found the horse when their dad came out of the house. We very nervously started telling him what happened.

"You're not going to have us hanged are you mister?" we asked.

He laughed and said, "No, but we have been looking for that horse everywhere. He got out of his pen and went way back on the property sounds like to me. You boys saved us a lot more looking."

Sheeewww! We were glad we weren't going to be hanged and glad to get out of there without going to jail. But, I tell you, we were two scared young boys.

Another Sibling

Soon, Mom gave birth to another baby. Another darned girl! We now had a little sister named Angela (Angie, we all called her). Darlene was really excited because now she had another girl to play with instead of playing dolls by herself. The family just seemed to keep growing.

The worst part of Mom having another baby was that each time, our grandmother (Mom's mom) thought she had to stay for several days to take care of us and to help Dad while mom was recuperating. She was a stern old woman and limited the amount of food we could have. We didn't have much to start with and she wouldn't even let us eat enough to get our bellies full. Seems she and Grandpa must not eat much, so that was how we were treated. She also tried to make Kenny and I do dishes. That wasn't gonna work!

I tell you, my dad had a *fit*. He told her in no uncertain terms that *his boys* were not going to work inside. They had plenty to do helping him take care of the farm. If she wanted help doing dishes, Darlene could help her. With that, he turned and ordered us out of the house and put us to work. That was the last time my grandmother ever stayed at our house. After that, when Mom needed help, the younger kids; Darlene, Darrell and Angie went to their house to stay, but Kenny and I stayed with Dad to take care of the chores.

When Mom wasn't able to take care of us, for whatever reason, Dad did his best, but he was certainly no cook. We had bologna sandwiches, made out of chunk bologna. Dad would cut a big slab of bologna and hand Kenny and I a slab about an inch thick. He would cut a thick piece of cheese and give it to us. We put them between two pieces of bread. We were doing exactly what Dad did. He would do the same, but his slab of bologna would be about two inches thick. He was a bigger guy, so he needed a bigger sandwich. That was lunch!

At night, he would fix these huge hamburgers for us. They were about a half pound a piece for me and Kenny. His hamburgers would be pushing the one pound mark. He didn't like them red in the middle and wanted them done, so he always ended up burning them. They were hard and burnt on one side and very dry on the other side. He must have used the entire saltshaker because they were so salty that we about choked on them. But, he tried and that was just Dad's way of getting a meal down us.

Come to think of it, I don't know that his cooking ever improved. When you are poor, you appreciate a meal, even a bad one. It was food and we didn't waste anything. Now, I would probably call it *roughing it,* but now that I think about it, it seemed as though back then, every day was roughing it to me.

When I was nine, my brother Lyle was born. Yet, another mouth to feed. We went through the whole *Dad cooking thing* again. When Dad was doing the cooking, the grocery shopping changed. Dad bought cheap sodas for us to drink, but to Kenny and me they were great. We never got soda any other time. Only when mom had a baby and the rest of the family went to stay with our grandparents for a couple of weeks. He also bought potato chips and dip. We were living high on the hog! Now and then he would even buy ice cream. That was a real treat.

Dad wouldn't wash any clothes, so we just wore the same ones every day. Clothes washin' and dish washin' was woman's work! After working in the barns around the livestock all day, our clothes not only stunk, but I swear our pants could stand up in a corner without us in them. Well, for a little while anyway!

Milk Cows

When Grandpa and Grandma Stanton came over, it was particularly nice. A visit from them was rare because we lived clear across the county from them. I loved my dad's parents. They were always so up-lifting. They were kind and loving with us kids. Even though they had a huge family, they were always all about family and loving each other. They just made me feel special.

We were really excited to see our grandparents, all of us kids were running around like crazy trying to talk to them. Grandpa had driven his truck that particular day and had a Jersey Milk Cow in the back. He said her name was Susie. Grandpa told Dad that he was giving us the milk cow because kids needed milk. With a milk cow it meant that we would be able to have milk on a regular basis and we could churn our own butter, make cottage cheese and even fresh cheese.

Susie was heavy with calf (that's pregnant in farm talk). Grandpa said when the calf was born that the calf was to belong to me and Kenny. He said we could start our own herd. We helped Grandpa and Dad get Susie off the truck and into the pasture. We worked with them to set up a stall for her in the barn.

A couple of weeks later, Susie had her calf. It was a beautiful little female calf. We named her Jeanie. It was interesting how, even though we had seen many calves born before on the farm, Jeanie was special. She was special because this one belonged to us and not the farmers Dad was working for. Suddenly, we were very interested in taking care of her.

We soon discovered something else; Susie wasn't like our beef cattle, which added yet another chore to our already long list. Susie had to be milked every morning and every evening. So, Dad took us into the stall and taught us how to milk. We were given this new chore. It was our responsibility. Every day, twice a day, we milked Susie by hand.

Dad began buying little calves that were not weaned yet because they were cheap. We were responsible for feeding them. We fed them powdered milk and we had to carry water to the barn to mix with the powder. We mixed it in a water bucket with a big nipple on it. Then, we would feed it to these calves until they were big enough to eat grass and hay.

Life was very busy. We were Dad's unpaid hired hands, Kenny and I. We got up early every morning, took care of the livestock, went to school, and when we came home from school, we would work with Dad in the fields. Then, we had to take care of the livestock again before going in for the night. We had no problem sleeping at night because we were exhausted.

Falling off the Tractor: My First Encounter with God

The spring before I turned eight, I was out on the tractor disking one warm sunny day. I had been disking all morning while Dad was off in another field plowing. Mom brought me out something to eat for lunch. It was a couple of biscuits and some fresh cow's butter.

It was really good. I ate those up and drank some water. I went right back to disking the field.

I had been out there so long that the old metal seat, which was so hard, made my butt start hurting. I pulled my jacket off and sat on it for a while, but even that got old and my butt was hurting again. So, like I had seen Dad do many times, I stood up and rode along looking back at the disk once in a while. All of a sudden, the tractor front tires hit a rock. It lurched and pushed the rock until the rock got stuck in the plowed ground. With a large bump, the tractor jumped over the rock. When it did, my foot slipped. Suddenly, I was falling back toward the disk. I knew what would happen if I fell into that disk. I was clawing the air; I knew I was about to die. My jacket sleeve was coming off the tractor seat where I had put it. Suddenly, it stuck under the bottom of the tractor seat.

It was as though someone guided and pushed my hand to that sleeve as it stuck in the crack of that metal bar. My feet were just dragging on the ground as the tractor kept going by itself and I dangled there for what seemed like forever. I was bruised and battered, but I pulled myself using all the strength I had back on that tractor. I got into the seat, pushed in the clutch and stopped the tractor. I put it in neutral and I just sat there. I was dazed. I had just been a split second from dying. The scene played over and over in my mind. WOW!

Then, I looked around to see if anyone was around because I had felt like someone had helped me out of that situation. I wanted to see if anyone was around to see what had happened. None! Not one person was within an eighth of a mile of me. There would have been no one to help me. If I had not been able to grab that jacket sleeve, if it hadn't gotten stuck in the metal bar that disk would have ran over me and cut me into a hundred pieces. I had seen what it had done to big hard clumps of clay.

I sat there on that tractor seat and thought back through what had just happened. There was no possible way I could have caught hold of that sleeve or the sleeve catch in that bar by itself, the way I was falling. It just didn't make sense how I had been saved. Even at that young age, I had a sense that someone was there. I looked around again, but once again I saw no one. Somehow, at that moment, I just knew God had spared me. We didn't really go to church, but I knew about God. I was sure it was Him.

I nervously put the tractor in gear and finished disking the field. When I was done, I went about refueling the tractor and getting it in the barn so I could grease the disk and get ready for the next day. I was reflecting back on my experience of the day and I decided I couldn't tell Dad or Mom about what happened to me that day. It just wouldn't be good. I wasn't sure they would understand that I felt someone had helped me when there was no one there. So, I never did tell them.

The Meeting in the Hay Field

A few days after the tractor incident, the weather had taken a real cold turn. It was early in May, but a cold front brought first, hail and then a snow that completely covered the ground. We had been having an unusually warm spring up to that day. The grass had greened and grown tall already for early May. So, we were surprised with the cold blast that followed.

Dad told me to go out to the hay field to see if the hay was tall enough to cut.

"When the weather turns cold like that, it traps more

nutrients up in the hay and makes it better for the cattle and sheep," said Dad.

I remember how cold it was when I headed out. I trudged through the snow toward the hay field. The hay field, Dad sent me to, was located up on a level piece of ground above the river bottoms. It had some really big hills coming off of the edges of it and then rolling down to the river bottoms. I liked to go out there. It was a solitary place where Kenny and I had previously found some Indian arrow heads. It was my kind of place.

Today was different. I had an overwhelming feeling that I just shouldn't be there. I walked out into the hay field through the snow a few feet. I was looking all around because I knew that Dad would not accept me just peering at it from the edge of the field. So, I walked deep into the hay field. I had to make sure that hay was tall enough in the middle of the field, too.

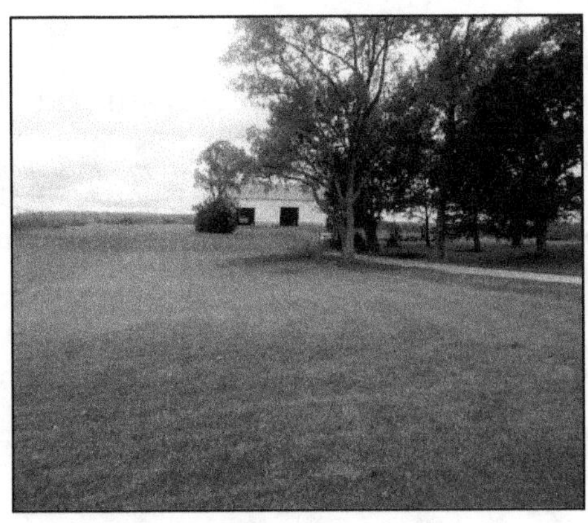

When I got toward the middle of the field, where it overlooked all the land below, there was a bright light shining down. Right there in the middle of all the snow was a circle that was very clear. There was no snow at all in this circle. Just beautiful green hay. I was surprised. As I stepped up to see what was going on with that particular spot, a voice spoke to me out of the heavens. It said, *Raymond, take the shoes off your feet, for this is Holy Ground.'*

I was scared and I had the feeling I wasn't worthy to be there. But, I did as I was directed. I took my shoes off and stepped into that light. I stepped onto the green hay in my bare feet. There was an instant warmth. It was like walking out of a freezer into a warm room. The warmth just radiated through my entire body. Even the ground felt warm on my bare feet. Then, I knelt down, it was as if I had to, I was just in awe. I could see the snow all around the outside, but in that small circle of light, it was warm.

Then, the voice spoke to me again. It said, *'I am going to use you in a mighty way. You will speak for me and I will work many miracles through you. I am preparing you to speak My word. Now go and tell no one what you have seen until I shall call you.'*

I had no doubt it was God that had spoken to me. Even though I had never been in church and I knew nothing about the Bible, I believed that God existed. I knew for certain I had just met Him.

I don't know how long I knelt there, but it was a long while. I didn't want to leave. I was in awe and scared at the same time. I had never felt warmth like this; never before. I felt such unconditional love toward me; it was indescribable.

When I finally came around, the light was gone. The circle remained warm for a good while. I stepped out of the circle and back into my shoes. I didn't want to get my feet wet. I remember that my shoes were so cold. They had been sitting in the snow.

When I got back down to the barn, Dad said, angrily, "Where have you been? Don't you know we have work to do? How tall was that hay? Is it tall enough to cut?"

I answered him very carefully. I could see he was angry and after what I had just been through, I didn't want a beating.

"Dad," I said, "I knew you wanted to know how tall the hay was all over the field, not just at the edges. So, I checked it all over. It's tall enough to get a good cutting."

"Oh, okay, well get busy helping your brother."

I did as I was told and I never did tell him about that encounter with God, but I never forgot.

The fact was, even as a nine-year-old-boy, I felt this big responsibility. I was always wondering when God would call.

When was this going to start? I didn't understand why I was chosen to receive this message. After all, I was just a kid and a very poor one at that. *Who was I? I was nothing.* A fear swept over me. I knew I wasn't worthy and I was afraid God would actually call. I was afraid I would not be able to complete the task that He had for me. I thought about it often, pondering what God was going to have me do. In a way, I think I was running from what God had for me. I didn't realize then how the devil would try to sow the seeds of doubt and fear in me.

Things Start to Change

At some point around the time we moved to the Kehrt Farm, my aunt Jenny contracted polio. She was very sick for what seemed like a long time. She died from her illness and left four young children. The youngest child was my cousin, Joe. Joe was only a few months old when his mother died. My uncle, Joe, was at a loss for what to do, so he sent the kids to my grandpa and grandma's house to live. It was a very hard time for him and all the family, for that matter.

My family took the two girls closest to my age in for a

while to help out. We kids had fun and we all tried to help out, but it made life pretty difficult adding more mouths to feed. Money was tight and there was never enough food.

After my aunt's death, my uncle had started drinking heavily. He would come over to visit his kids. He was always very kindhearted and I thought a lot of Uncle Joe, but he would sit at our house and drink. Eventually, my dad started drinking with him. I had never seen my dad drunk until then. Eventually, Dad started drinking all the time. As I look back now, I think he was trying to drink away the situation we were in. When Dad drank, he would get mean.

Uncle Joe came by one day with a table saw he was trying to sell to my dad. It was a small saw, but it worked well. Dad really didn't need it and we absolutely had no money to spare, but I think he felt sorry for Uncle Joe and he liked it, so he bought it anyway. We set it up in the barn and Dad played around with sawing some boards. He taught Kenny and me how to use it. The lesson came with a stern warning that we could only use it when he was with us.

Well, boys will be boys and one day when Dad was on the back of the property inspecting a field, we took advantage of the free time. We decided to make sling shot rifles like the one a boy on TV was shooting. We worked and worked but needed to cut them. So, I turned on the saw and made the first gun and gave it to Kenny. It worked great! Kenny was shooting rocks all over the place.

It was my turn. I started making my slingshot rifle. I started working on it and when I got to the part where it needed to be cut, I turned on the saw like I had before. Everything was going great, when suddenly the saw hit a knot in the board. The board snapped forward and threw my left hand right into the saw blade. It happened so fast. My hand hit the blade bounced a couple of times and I quickly pulled it back.

I looked at my fingers in disbelief. The little finger on my left hand fell off to the side; it was just hanging by a piece of skin. The one next to it was mangled. The middle finger was missing the very tip and there was blood flowing everywhere. I yelled for Kenny, grabbed my left hand and we ran to the house. As soon as I got in the house, I yelled for Mom. She hurriedly came to see what was going on. I could tell by the look on her face it was bad. She put on a brave front, but there was absolute panic and horror in her eyes. She held my hand under the faucet and ran cold water on it to wash the blood off.

Finally, she was able to see the mangled mess that had been my three fingers. The little one kept falling off to the side. I put it back in place and held it there. Mom must have gotten queasy because she almost fell to the floor. She maintained her composure and sent Kenny running for Dad.

A few minutes later Dad came in; he took one look. He said, "We have to go to the doctor, now!"

The drive into the doctor's office was quick, but I think the reason I remained calm was probably because I was in shock. Mom stayed home because of the littler kids. It was me, Kenny and Dad. Kenny was crying in the back seat.

"It will be ok, Kenny. It will take a long time to heal, but everything will be ok," I said.

I never even cried. Instead, I had this strange sense of peace that overwhelmed me.

When we arrived at the doctor's office, the nurse took one look at me and knew what was happening. She knew this was bad! The doctor took me right back. When I unwrapped my hand, he touched the fingers to inspect the damage. Upon his touch, the little pinky finger fell off to the side again.

"He's lost the little one, part of another one and will lose the other one down to the middle knuckle. We need to get him to the hospital NOW! I will have a surgeon at the hospital waiting for you. We can't waste any time," Dad said.

Dad drove us quickly to the hospital. When we arrived, there were people already waiting for us outside the emergency room. They rushed me into surgery.

The staff was very kind. As they started the IV, one of them said, "Okay, cowboy, we are going to take care of you."

The Surgeon came in and inspected my fingers.

"You are going to be able to save them, right?" I asked.

"I can't make any promises, but I will try my best."

When I woke up after the surgery, the surgeon was there in the room.

"I tried to save your fingers. I reattached the little one and reconstructed what I could of the other two. We will see what happens over the next couple of days. If they start turning black they will have to come off," he said.

That surgeon's name was Doctor Inlow. He and I became good friends before that ordeal was over. He told me it took over six hundred stitches to sew me up.

When I got home from the hospital, my uncle, Joe, came over to the house, came upstairs to my bedroom and talked with me.

"If I had known you would have gotten hurt like this, I would have never sold that saw to your dad," he said.

I heard a tremor in his voice and he had tears in his eyes when he said it. I noticed that he had to turn his head away from me for a little while.

Dad stood in the background and said, "I told you boys not to mess with that saw."

Dad never really jumped on me about it, but when the bills came in, I sure heard about it.

It took over a year of whirlpool baths on my hand and physical therapy before I would be released from Doctor Inlow's care. During that year he and I had a lot of great conversations. I found out that he had just completed his residency a short while before the accident. He was a top-notch surgeon. I found out later that almost anyone else in town would have just taken the fingers off. He had just learned the technique that allowed him to reattach the fingers. He had to bypass veins and the nerve endings. He saved my fingers. I lost the tip of the middle one. It is still shorter than the others, but after a year of pain, healing and talking to Dr. Bob, I was doing well. The last joint of my little finger was still stiff, but I was not one to complain after all I had been through.

Many years later, after I was grown, I stopped by my Aunt Mary's house in Shelbyville, Indiana one day just to visit. While we talked, the subject of my hand came up.

She told me that after Dad had left the hospital the day I cut my fingers all up, that he had come to her house. She said when he came in she could see that something was wrong. When he told her what had happened, she said he broke down and cried. That was the only time she saw him cry and I never had.

She told me that He said I had been the bravest kid he had ever seen. That stuck with me for the rest of my life. Dad never praised us for anything but he would tell other people how proud he was of us.

A New Brother

When I was ten, my mom had her last baby, they named him Chris. Wow! Did we have a house full! Not only were there lots of hungry days with so many mouths to feed, but we also didn't have enough beds. Kenny and I shared a bed. Darlene and Angela shared a bed. Then Darrel, Lyle and now Chris would share a bed. Times were hard, but we were a family.

The Ice Trip Down River

The days always seemed as though they flew by. We were always so busy; work, work, and more work. We had to stay busy or starve. Those were the alternatives. If we didn't have enough wood, we had to get out in the cold and cut wood or freeze. Dad never seemed to realize that he needed to prepare for winter before winter got there. We were always forced to cut wood when it was freezing outside. It would have been nice if he had been a little more prepared so we didn't have to work outside in the worst weather.

Dad had made Kenny and I our own axes. They had a shorter handle on them than his did. It wasn't something he did special for us, it was so we could work alongside him. Now, we could help cut limbs from trees while Dad cut the tree up. We could also help split the wood.

One exceptionally cold winter day, I remember there was snow about two feet and drifts even deeper. Dad discovered we were out of firewood. So, we bundled up and hooked up the tractor and trailer. We drove back to the woods. The snow was so deep, we ended up cutting trees on the edge of a riverbank. We were dropping them on the ice so we could cut them up and carry them up the bank to load them in the trailer.

Dad would cut a tree down. It would slide down the bank on to the ice. Kenny and I would walk out on the frozen river to "limb the tree", we called it. Dad was cutting the trees up and we were limbing them out.

The ice we were walking on was close to very fast water. It was flowing much too fast to freeze. So, I directed Kenny to stand back closer to the stronger ice. I was trying to protect him just in case the ice was thin where I was going to walk. I was working on the side of the tree where the majority of the limbs were. Kenny was already finished with his section. While Dad was cutting the tree up into sections, Kenny got bored. He started chopping at the ice. He was just playing around when all of a sudden the piece I was standing on broke free from the ice sheet. He had chopped enough around me that suddenly, I was floating down stream on a piece of ice.

I tried to balance myself, but it wasn't long before the piece of ice I was standing on hit a rock. Down into the water I fell. I did not know how to swim. My first thought was that I was going to die. I knew I was a goner. The water was so cold that when I fell in, it took my breath away. I came up gasped for air and went under again being pulled down river and then miraculously, I felt my feet hit something. It was a gravel bar just under the water. Somehow I had been pushed right up to it. I climbed up on it and gasping for air. I tried to clear the water out of my throat and fought to breathe.

I was soaking wet and instantly when the wind hit me, it was even colder than it had been in the water. I looked around the riverbank and saw Dad and Kenny running through the snow drifts trying to get to me. I made my way to what seemed to be the easiest area to climb up the bank onto dry land. I was so cold and the snow was so deep, I just couldn't get my legs and arms to move right. It was like I was moving in slow motion. The cold and the water had sapped all the strength out of me. Dad made it to the bank directly above me and said, "Climb or you will freeze to death."

I gave it one last effort and this time I was just out of Dad's reach. He held a big limb down the bank for me to grab hold of. I was able to get my hands around the limb and he pulled me up onto the top of the bank. My clothes were frozen. He started rubbing snow on me and quickly worked to build a fire.

He tried and tried, but couldn't get the fire going. He finally gave up and loaded me on the tractor. We rushed me to the house. I remember sitting by the fire and my mom started pouring hot tea down my throat. She kept urging me to drink more and more. Dad had to go back out and get the wood that we had cut. He brought it back up to the house as soon as he could so we could keep the fire going.

As I started to warm up, the pain began first; my fingers and then my hands and feet then my arms and legs. They felt like they were on fire as they started to warm up from the hypothermia.

I remember, later, sitting in the living room by the fire and I heard Dad tell Mom, "That kid has nine lives. I thought for sure he was gone." I remember Mom saying, "Well, I think God has His hands on him."

The Stanton's Get Guns!

That next Christmas we were really struggling. Financially, it was a strain with so many mouths to feed. Once again, we had not cut enough wood to heat the house for the long, hard winter. The cold also made it rough on the livestock. But, in our lives, the livestock always came first. They brought in the money that supported the family. Kenny and I were used to getting perhaps one present each. Sometimes, we got some hard candy and a few nuts or if we were really lucky an orange.

This Christmas, we had been going back and forth to the elevator pulling wagon loads of corn behind the tractors. I even drove the old 1948 dodge one and a half ton truck to the elevator with a few loads of corn. Dad was busy in the fields running the corn picker.

To a couple of farm boys, the elevator was a neat place. We always had to pull the load onto the scales, unload it and then go inside to pick up our receipt for the load. While we were inside, we would talk to the old guys in the office.

They would ask, "Did you bring that load by yourself?"

"Yep," I always answered.

"Really?" they questioned me.

I think they thought it was neat that a young boy would be bringing the load of corn all by himself.

There were always peanuts in a big barrel in the grain office. Kenny and I would shell and eat peanuts and we would almost always ask if we could take some for later. "Sure," they always said. We would load our pockets full and give them to the little ones and to mom.

Just before Christmas, they always had a supply of hard Christmas candy in the elevator office. The old guys always gave all of the farmers, who came in on a regular basis, a can of candy. They treated Kenny and I just like the adult farmers and gave us each a can. We were elated, driving those tractors back home that day.

So, this particular Christmas we had low expectations. We

knew there wasn't much money. But, like all kids back then, we looked through the sears catalog making wishes. We weren't even sure that we would get anything this year. The year before we had gotten corn cobs. Corn cobs!! Really!! Dad said it was because we had been bad. That was such a huge disappointment. Kenny cried and literally threw a fit. I was just mad. But, at the same time, I understood that the real reason was that there just wasn't enough money. Mom and Dad felt the little kids needed a little something more than us; we were older boys. We were old enough to realize just how hard things were.

We always cut our own Christmas tree from the woods. That Christmas morning all the little kids got up and rushed in around the Christmas tree. Kenny even rushed in, but I just took my time. I was told to start passing out the kid's gifts, so I got under the tree and started pulling out gifts one-by-one and handing them out. I felt disappointment come over me, but I tried to keep my spirits up.

There was a doll for Darlene, a little tea set for Angela, and some little plastic toy tractors for the little boys. When I turned back to the tree, I noticed that was all. Everything was gone. Kenny just stood there looking at the empty space under the tree with this look of absolute despair on his face. He looked over at me and I just knew he was going to cry.

Dad turned to us and said, "Boys, Mom and I got something for you, but it wasn't something we could put under the tree. I was still sitting there under the tree. I still had this sinking feeling that it wasn't going to be much. Just another disappointing Christmas. I was almost getting used to them.

Dad went into the other room and came out with two big, long boxes. He handed one to Kenny and brought me one. *Wow! It was heavy!* In the back of my mind I thought, *it's probably bricks or something.* Kenny ripped the wrapping paper off his box; I saw the picture of a rifle.

"*Whoa!*" I thought, "*Hey, a BB Gun. That's great because ours was broken and we were told it cost too much to get it fixed.*" So, I found myself getting a little more excited. I opened my present and, sure enough, there was that picture of a rifle.

Kenny tore his box open and yelled, "It's a BB Gun!"

I opened my box; I took the gun out. It felt too heavy for a BB gun. The barrel was a heavy metal, not like the thin barrel of a Daisy Red Rider.

I yelled to Kenny, "Yours might be a BB gun, but mine is a real rifle."

It was an Ithaca 22 caliber Saddle gun, just like the cowboys use on TV. *Well almost.* It wasn't a repeating rifle, and it was a lot smaller caliber. But, *I HAD A REAL RIFLE.* Kenny's was the same thing, only with a little lighter colored stock. We were two excited boys!

We also got a box of shells each. Dad took us outside and spent time with us making sure we knew how to shoot them. We had to aim carefully. We found out, unlike the bb's in a BB Gun, the 22 caliber could travel about a mile. Dad said we had to make sure we knew where that bullet was going to end up before we fired.

That winter, we enjoyed going hunting as much as possible. We always had to ask Dad first. We brought home squirrels and rabbits. They weren't a big meal, but they did help feed us. Mom was always happy to see us bring them in. Dad never would eat them, but Mom would fix them for us kids. I never did really know why he wouldn't eat rabbit or squirrel. He always seemed to have a particular love of animals, maybe that's why.

Putting Hay in the Barn

We were used to hard work, as I mentioned before, and bailing hay each year was nothing new. Spent many summers baling hay, but this year we had an abundance of hay. We had also lucked into obtaining some hay from some surrounding farms. As the farm grew, we were getting more and more livestock. We bought several more beef cattle and even a few sheep, so the hay was important.

This year, Dad decided to have my older cousin, Glen come over and help us for a few days. I was about ten, and Glen was about 6 years older than me. Glen loved to climb. He would walk up the elevator to the hayloft instead of going into the barn. He preferred going up the ladder. The elevator sat at an angle and was raised as high as it could be in order to reach the big doorway located in the upper part of the hay loft.

Dad would unload the wagon loads of hay by throwing the bales unto the elevator and it would bring the bales up to the big open doorway. We would catch the bales and stack them as neatly as we could in the loft. By stacking them neatly, it enabled us to get as much hay in the loft as possible. When we were finished emptying the wagons we would all climb down and go back out to the field to load the wagons again.

Glen would just wait until the elevator was shut off, then he would walk down the elevator right out to the wagon and away he would go. It was cool to Kenny and me, so we started doing it, too. At first, it was pretty scary because it was definitely higher than I liked to be above the ground. We were out on a little piece of metal, but I was determined. I did it. It became routine for us and we got faster at it. Doing it more quickly gave us a few more minutes of rest before we had to work again.

That evening, after Glen went home, Kenny and I continued using the elevator up and back down from the lofts. One day, as we finished unloading the hay, Dad took off with the wagon and we were left in the loft stacking the last few bales. I started out the door high above the ground. I stepped out onto the elevator like I always did, but what I didn't realize was the elevator had shifted a little and the top of it wasn't resting on the floor of the loft. Since it was on wheels, it slid and with my weight on it, it dropped about a foot throwing me off balance.

I started falling. I was barely able to catch the side of it with one hand. There I was dangling high above the ground. With some effort, I was able to get my other hand on the side of the elevator, but every time I would move, the elevator would tip and start to fall. It slid further and further away from the barn. I couldn't reach the barn loft and I couldn't move for fear of it tipping the elevator over and me with it.

Once again, I believe God was watching out for me. Miraculously, the wheel on the elevator jammed against a rock. It acted like a chock for the wheel. I mustered up enough strength to pull myself up just enough so that I could get my leg over the edge. I was trying very carefully to not move too far or too fast so the wheel wouldn't jar away from that rock. Slowly, deliberately, I worked my way toward the ground.

When I was safe on the ground, out of breath and with my heart about to burst out of my chest, thoughts of just how close I had come to being seriously injured or even killed by that fall ran through my head. I muttered, "**Thank you God**."

I never told Dad about the incident. Kenny had seen the whole thing from the loft. It scared him enough that he decided he would go down the ladder from now on.

Killing Chickens

Kenny and I had started helping Mom kill a chicken once in a while to eat since we were four or five years old. It was no surprise when Mom had started asking us to do the killing by ourselves. She never did like to do it. Neither did we, for that matter, but, hey you have to eat! I knew that after we killed that chicken and Mom cooked it, it was going to taste good.

Remember, I said before that Dad had made us shorter handled axes? We used those axes to kill the chickens. We started by laying their necks on a block of wood and chopping off their head with our axe. One day, my grandma (on Mom's side), said it was much easier to hang them over the metal clothesline and take a sharp knife and cut their heads off. That sounded sensible, so we tried it. While it was quicker, it was more difficult for us boys. When you kill a chicken, they tend to flop around. Cutting their heads off this way caused them to throw blood all over you as they flopped around. It was a nasty bloody mess!

One day, Mom called us down from the barn and said, "Boys, I want you to kill me four chickens."

"Okay Mom, which ones do you want killed?"

She pointed out four older chickens that weren't laying eggs.

Kenny turned to me after Mom had walked away and said, "Dog-gone-it! I hate having to chase those chickens down and then cut their heads off with a knife."

"Kenny, Mom said to kill them, she didn't say how we had to kill them," I said.

Kenny smiled a great big smile at me when he saw the glint in my eyes.

"What are we going to do, then?" Kenny asked.

"Let's separate them out in the chicken yard, pen the others in the coop, and shoot them."

"Oh, yeah, that sounds better."

I told him we have to shoot them in the head though or Mom will be mad. So, we penned the other chickens up and took out our trusty rifles. We took aim. We were getting better and better at shooting and it was almost like second nature to us. I dropped the first chicken with one shot. It didn't know what hit it, thank goodness! It dropped and flopped a little, like chickens do, but it was dead. Then Kenny shot one.

Mom came running out of the house yelling, "You boys can't shoot those chickens. I don't want bullets in the meat."

"Mom, we are only shooting them in the head. Look, it's a lot more humane than the knife," I said.

"Okay, let's see."

I took aim; down went another one. Then, Kenny dropped the other one. We had four just like Mom wanted.

"Go get them and let's just make sure that you didn't get bullets in the meat," Mom said.

When we brought them up to the house, there were four chickens shot through the head. We were pretty proud. But, after that, we always just went out and shot any chickens Mom wanted. We had another new chore!

Hunting to Survive

When I was about ten years old, Dad acquired a self-propelled combine. It was an Allis Chalmers Gleaner E. It was great. That combine helped us get a better price for our crops because it sifted more of the weeds and seeds from the grain. It also shelled the corn instead of only picking the ears. As Dad would shell corn, I would stand out on the ladder walkway with my gun watching for rabbits. While he got the hopper full, I was looking for dinner.

We would occasionally startle a rabbit and it would take off. I would aim and shoot them with my 22 rifle. It was a good way to add meat for the freezer. The younger kids were getting bigger; they were starting to eat more and more. It helped put food on our table.

Kenny and I got into the habit of carrying our rifles with us when we went back to the woods to bring the cows up to milk. If we saw a squirrel or a rabbit, we would shoot it and bring it home to Mom. When you are hungry, every shot counts when it meant eating or doing without, so we got to be really good shots.

Hauling Corn

hen I was in the fifth grade, we started hauling corn because of a suggestion made to my dad. Dad went to the elevator one day and the guys who owned it said, "Bob, if you had a newer truck we could use you to haul corn for us."

So, Dad drove into town and talked to the banker and next thing we knew he had a 1965 Ford F500 ton and a half truck.

We started hauling corn for all the farmers around the area who didn't have trucks or were too old to haul it themselves. Unfortunately, that didn't get us out of work. We still had all the work to do on our place; milk the cows, take care of the livestock, plow and disk; plant; cultivate and harvest our crops. Only now, we were also hauling corn.

Hauling corn meant we had to shovel ears of corn out of a corn crib and into an elevator. It was back-breaking work. The amount of corn-hauling we did grew and grew and along with that came more and more work. Now, Dad had a truck payment and had to buy fuel. He was also making payments on the combine he had bought earlier.

He still seemed to come up short. So, he started combining for other farmers. Even with this extra work, we still weren't making enough money to pay for all of the expenses. That spring, we started plowing and disking and planting for other farmers, too.

My dad just wasn't a good businessman. I discovered later that he wasn't charging other farmers enough to cover his own expenses. There was fuel and also the wear on the equipment. There just wasn't enough of a profit margin and he had borrowed money for the equipment. If Dad was working harder and harder, that meant Kenny and I were working like borrowed mules.

Plus, during this time, Dad was drinking all the time. He would pick up a six-pack of beer whenever he was around a town with a bar or liquor store. He would drink in the truck as we were going home. He would take a drink and then pass the beer over to me and I would pass it to Kenny and back to Dad. The circle repeated until we arrived home.

When we would get home, I would jump out of the truck and open the barn doors. Dad would back in and then he would sit and drink the rest of the beer. Dad told us we had to sit there with him until he was done so Mom wouldn't complain. It was not a good situation to put two young boys in.

A Horse of Our Own

The summer between my fifth and sixth grade years, we were baling a lot of hay. It was still early in the summer and the old bailer broke down. We took it apart and tried to fix it, but it was done. It just wasn't worth putting the money into. So, while we were working out in the fields, Dad made some calls and got someone to come out and finish bailing our hay.

When we came in, Dad gave us our instructions. He said, "Boys a guy is coming here tomorrow to bale that hay. I have to haul a load of corn. You boys get up early in the morning and get the milking done and feed the stock. Then, I want you to get your butts up to the house in time to meet that guy. You help load the wagons just the way we always do".

When Dad told us to do something, we knew we had better do it. We either did what he told us, or we paid the price. He was drinking all the time now, which meant a beating with the belt if we didn't listen. And it would be a beating that we wouldn't forget for a week or two.

That night, I couldn't hardly sleep. I knew I had to get Kenny up extra early so we could get the chores done and be ready to meet the guy who was baling our hay. I did manage to get up early. I had everything organized and got done with the chores in plenty of time and the guy still hadn't arrived. We went ahead and pulled the hay wagons around to the field and had them sitting in the right area. This would make it easier because we could fill up all of the wagons. There wouldn't be any need to stop bailing until they were all full. Then, we could take the hay up to the barn.

Finally, the guy showed up with a brand new pickup truck pulling a brand new bailer. We were in awe! Man, it was a nice rig. That Chevy pickup was the most beautiful thing I had ever seen.

He got out of the truck and said, "Hi, boys. Where's your dad?"

"He had to haul some corn. He won't be back until this evening," we answered.

He was none too happy about that. He got this angry look on his face.

"Well, I'm supposed to bale hay for him today. Where is all my help?"

"You're looking at 'em," I said.

"What!" he said, raising his voice.

"My brother and I are going to do all the loading. You just have to bale."

"There is no way you two young boys can keep up with me. You are too young."

"Well, we do it all of the time. You just do the baling. You don't worry about us. We will take care of the rest."

He was mad!

"Where is the field?" he asked.

"Right back here."

I led the way, opening the gates for him as he drove through. When he got back to the field, he saw the wagons arranged.

"Who did that?"

"I did it earlier this morning."

"Well, why do you have them set out like that?"

"So we don't have to stop until we have them all loaded."

He kind of muttered a, *Hmmmph* under his breath.

"Okay, we will try it out, but if you two can't keep up, I will shut it down and charge your dad for my time."

"Oh," I said, "We will keep up."

We worked all day. He was baling and we loaded the wagons as fast as we could hustle. At the end of the day, he pulled off his cowboy hat, wiped the sweat off his forehead and just looked at us.

"Boys, I tell you what, you two are workers. I will give you that. When I get back here tomorrow, are you going to have those wagons ready to go again?"

"Yep, of course we are. They will be ready."

He shook his head and laughed a little.

"See you early tomorrow."

Kenny and I worked way into the night getting that hay in the barn loft, but we got it all in there. Early the next morning, we went into the next hay field and placed the wagons just as we had done the day before.

We found out the guy's name was Levi. When he came over the next day, he said, "Are you boys ready?"

"Yep," we replied.

This time there was a big smile on his face. We went at it again. We only stopped for a half hour at noon.

During our break, we asked him about his nice truck.

"Sure is a nice truck, mister."

"I raise quarter horses and made money baling hay and trading horses."

Now, we loved horses, so he had our attention when he told us about those horses.

"We always wanted a horse, but they cost way too much money," we said.

We headed back to work and Levi worked with us all that day. In fact, he worked with us the rest of the summer. Because our baler was broke, he did all our baling for us. We got to be good friends with him. He even came over and picked us up one afternoon to take us to his horse farm and show us around. I couldn't believe Dad let us go, but he did. We had a great time riding horses.

We worked our way through the winter and our friend, Levi, moved on from our lives. Spring was coming on strong. We hadn't seen Levi in a while, but one day he showed up at our house in that nice pickup truck. He was pulling a horse trailer. We were excited to see him. We dropped everything and went running out to say hello to our friend. He stepped out of the truck and was all smiles.

"Hey boys, you know I been thinking about you boys. I remember you said you were needing a horse and I just decided to bring you one."

We couldn't believe our ears! He walked us around to the back of the trailer and there was a little quarter horse colt.

"This one is a little smaller than the ones I usually sell so, I want you two boys to have him."

We were ecstatic! We named our new horse, Cimarron. He was a beautiful colt and we spent all of our extra time, which was never enough, with him. We would curry comb and brush him. He was definitely a spoiled horse. Kenny and I were horse owners.

We also had our own milk cow. Jeanie, our cow, had grown up before our eyes and was expecting her first calf. We watched her with anticipation, as her time came to birth her calf. The day came and we were excited that it was a little bull calf. He was a rowdy little guy. We were pretty happy kids. We had a horse, a cow and a bull calf. Well, we were happy, until Dad told us we were going to have to help pay for the feed for our animals.

I was a little disappointed that we would have to do more work and the money would go to our animals, but I thought about it for a little while.

"Well, now we have another cow that gives us milk, so that helps to put food on the table. I think that should even things out for their keep. We should make enough off of the cow to pay for the feed for the other two, as well," I told dad.

As the calf grew, it became obvious to me that Dad had plans to sell him. He grew fast and before I knew it, he was around 600 pounds. Dad worked a deal with us and sold the calf. The deal was that Dad would give us $50. And to be honest, we never got the $50.00. We knew the family had to eat. The deal was Dad didn't sell the calf, so he didn't end up on someone else's table. But, he did end up on ours!

Acting Like Men

Most of our days consisted of work. So, school became our get-away. It was a place of learning, but we also had recess. Recess was the best! We played games with our friends. Now, once in a while, we would get into a fight with other kids, but it was usually just wrestling around. We spent most of our time trying to act like a man instead of being boys. We were trying to be just like Dad.

As I look back now, it was not a proper upbringing. Kenny and I were drinking beer with Dad. By the time I was about nine, I could cuss like a sailor. I had a foul mouth and used it most of the time. I'm not even sure I realized how bad it sounded. It was just a normal part of life to me.

School was okay. I had made friends. It wasn't a big school and I knew every kid in the entire elementary school. When I started the seventh grade, I had to choose what Junior high school to attend. Both schools as an option were 7th through 12th grades.

Since it was my decision, I chose the school located closest to the farm.

Jr. High School

The Junior High I chose was in the town of Waldron, near where I lived. I had been there a few times at the bank or to get gas for the truck. I was excited and went into that first day with this expectation that I would be "a Jock." I was surprised, and not pleasantly! It was a big school.

I was a lowly 7th grader and running up and down stairs with the bigger high school students could be a dangerous thing. We had very little time to get from class to class. I noticed those big guys would climb three steps at a time and just jump down from landing to landing. I have to say, I was impressed.

It so happened, I had a study hall class in the library. By the time I got in there, I had to sit with a bunch of junior and senior guys. I was there for my study hall class. Those guys were there because they were in trouble and had, most likely, been kicked out of class. It didn't take long before I fit right in. They taught me the fine art of shooting spit balls. We shot them at the teacher in the library and at each other. I already talked like them because every other word I said was a cuss word, so I fit right in.

One of them asked me, "Are you going to the cafeteria

for lunch?"

"Yeah!"

"We don't eat that crap. We go downtown for lunch."

"Really? You mean we can do that?"

"Sure," they said, "Come on."

Boy, I thought I was something. I'm just a 7th grader and I'm running around with the older guys.

We went downtown to this little restaurant. I got a cheap sandwich, I think. After we left the restaurant, one guy went into the grocery store and picked up a pack of cigarettes. They offered me a smoke, so I lit one up. They were a little surprised that I knew how to smoke, but I'd had plenty of practice.

My twin uncles, who were ten years older than I was, taught me how to smoke early-on. They made me smoke with them so I wouldn't rat them out to Grandpa. *Guilty by association!* The high school guys were impressed.

"Hey, this little guy is cool. He's one of us."

From that point on, I was one of the cool guys. We always went out together for lunch.

One afternoon, as I headed to my next class, my friend Duke said, "Hey, Stanton we're all going to the hayfield for a drag race. You going?"

"You mean after school?" I asked.

"No, right now. You going or not?"

"Sure!" I said and out the door we went.

We jumped a fence and into a waiting car. Away we went! There were two carloads of guys who were racing each other. They were chasing each other through the country. After a while, we turned off the road into a huge, flat, hayfield. The two cars lined up and everyone except the drivers, crawled out. They were arguing back and forth over who should officially 'start' the race.

Someone shouted, "Hey, little Stanton, you start it."

I had no idea how to start a race. Duke gave me a quick overview while everyone else was placing bets on who would win. They lined up and I started the race. All went well. After that, I was always the official race starter for the guys.

Unfortunately, I got all wound up in what was going on and I missed the school bus home. I was worried. Dad would kick my butt all over the place if I wasn't home to do my chores.

"Ah, don't worry about it. We will get you home before the bus makes it there," my friend Duke said.

The guys took me close, but not all the way home, and dropped me off. I stood there patiently and waited for the bus to pull up with my brother. When Kenny got off the school bus, I ran around behind the bus and then came up right beside him as if I had gotten off the bus, too, and was waiting for him. He was never the wiser.

It was pretty exciting running with the older guys. It made me feel older than I was. I was the starter for all of the races. I was also included when the guys went cruising. I knew most of their girlfriends and they started fixing me up with their younger girlfriends. Now, the seventh grade girls were even more interested than before. Now I was cool!

The Farm Sells

I remember, one day when I got in from school, Dad gave me the usual run-down on what he wanted done that day. He added some extra work that particular day.

"The lady who owns this farm called me and wants me to come into town to talk to her," he said.

So, I had Dad's chores to do, too, that day. He took off and Kenny and I did the work he assigned to us. He was gone a really long time. Finally, Dad came home drunk: three-sheets-to-the-wind, as they say today.

"Mrs. Kehrt is going to sell the farm. She says she is just getting too old to worry with it anymore," Dad said.

We were all in shock.

"Well, how much is she asking for it?" Mom said.

"Seventy-five thousand dollars."

In today's terms, that would be the equivalent to five-hundred and fifty thousand dollars. Mom was hoping we could buy the farm, but I knew that it was an impossible amount for my dad to come up with. They had hoped they could buy it, so he and Mom talked about it. They devised a plan to speak to Mrs. Kehrt to convince her to sell them the farm on contract.

Dad made another trip into town to talk with her. Mrs. Kehrt was a very nice lady, but she was also a businesswoman. She would love to have sold us the farm, but deep down, she knew Dad wouldn't be able to afford it. She had to refuse the contract offer Dad gave her.

Dad went the next day and talked to several different bankers in town, but no one was willing to loan him the money. As a last-ditch effort, he heard about a government backed loan for farmers, but it took several months to get those approved. He applied anyway. Before we had a chance to hear anything about the loan, we received word that Mrs. Kehrt's nephew bought the farm.

We were told we needed to get the crops harvested and sell the livestock. We would split the proceeds before the end of the year. I remember Dad was devastated. He tried not to show it, but he wanted that old farm and it just didn't happen. He started drinking more than ever because of the disappointments in his life. Kenny and I were doing more and more of the work that needed done.

My dad was always a procrastinator. This disappointment made it worse. When the time was almost up for us to leave, Mrs. Kehrt's nephew extended our stay on the farm by a couple more weeks. He told us after those two weeks then that was it, he would take possession of the farm.

We only had two weeks to get those crops in so we could have money. Dad called on my uncles to come and help. We managed to get the crops in and sold, we sold our animals. Dad's share wasn't much, but it paid the bills for the equipment and we had a little extra to live on. Still yet, we had to move and we had no place to go.

At the last minute, Mom and Dad found a farm near Indianapolis that was hiring a farm hand. Dad talked to the big old German lady and her little skinny old husband. The old guy was a decent sort, but the woman was a bossy, demanding, great big old woman who was used to telling people what to do.

Dad told them about the deal we had with Mrs. Kehrt farming for half of the crops, but that old woman was smart enough that she realized if the crops were poor that year she would be far ahead with Dad's plan than if she kept all the crops and just paid someone a salary. If the crops were good, she would do even better. Dad agreed to the deal and we moved onto their 330 acre farm.

This move was a bigger job than the last time we moved because we now had three tractors, a combine and all the other farm equipment Dad had accumulated. We also had a horse, two cows and now there were seven of us kids. Plus, we had all of our general stuff; furniture, clothes, toys, kitchen stuff, etc. It was a massive move.

We were moving just outside of Indianapolis on a major highway. We had to drive our equipment up that road. It was difficult, not to mention hazardous at times. The farm was split on both sides of the highway. Some of the equipment had to go across the highway, so we had to cross traffic. When working the farm, we constantly had to cross the road.

The house was backed up to a long tree-lined lane. The lane was a half-mile back. We drove passed the old lady's house, who owned the farm. Then, passed by the barns and then, finally, there was our house. It was not nearly as nice as the land-owners' house, but that was to be expected. It was also half as big as our last house. It did have something we had never had before. When we walked in, there was a bathroom with a flushing toilet, a sink and a bathtub.

Wow! We were excited enough about that bathroom, but when we headed upstairs to see our rooms, there was another even bigger bathroom. We always used an outhouse before. When we finally got a bathroom in a house, in fact, we got two. We were really stepping up in the world.

Life started out busy and stayed busy at this new farm. Not only did we have our two cows to milk, but we ended up with the twenty-four other milk cows that the old lady had. We had to milk those cows, too. Dad also bought a bunch of pigs for us to take care of. The old lady and her husband had 60 head of beef cattle that we were responsible for. That was part of the deal for us living on the farm.

Each morning, we were up before dawn to begin milking the milk cows. In those days, all of the milking was done by hand. I distinctly remember, for the first several weeks, feeling like my arms were just going to explode. They hurt so badly. My hands would cramp up and my fore arms were swollen.

Sometimes, I felt I could barely get through the day. We finished the morning milking, had other chores or school and then at 5 o'clock in the evening, we started milking all over again. It was torture. But, it had to be done. Those cows had to be milked. We made money from selling the milk. Over a period of time, as the winter wore on, I slowly got used to it. My hands still became sore and arms ached, but it was not as painful.

The New School

The biggest shock after the move was the new Junior High School. I was kind of excited about it because it actually had a football team and I had always wanted to play football.

The moment we walked into that school, I could tell that the principal and the teachers were different than anything I had experienced before. The teachers in the small rural farm area schools I had previously attended were genuinely interested in helping the kids learn.

The principal and the teachers at this new school were very condescending to my mother and not at all happy that we were there. They acted as though they were going to help us but they were smirking and looking down on us. Even as a young man, I could tell they were lying when they said they would help us get acclimated to the new school. From the very beginning, I had a very uneasy feeling about the situation.

As I got settled into my classes, I started to notice big differences in the way the other kids acted. They were suburban kids and we were farm

kids. Most of these kids had been in big schools in big cities like Indianapolis. One of the first things I noticed is that they weren't dressed like I was. It seemed we were from two totally different worlds and lived completely different lives. They went home after school and rode their bikes and played. We went home and worked on the farm late into the evening.

One day, as I was sitting at my desk, a kid came up and grabbed me by the jaw and squeezed real hard.

"Give me your lunch money… NOW… or I will have my friends kick your ass," he said.

He motioned to his friends who stepped forward. They were great big kids who must have failed at least a couple of grades.

"I'm the one who runs the seventh grade," the kid said.

Well, that didn't work for me. I was strong enough that instinctively I reached up grabbed his wrist and squeezed as hard as I could. All that cow milking gave me one heck of a grip. Within seconds, I dropped him to the floor. He was yelling for me to let go.

He yelled and said, "My friends will get you!"

Being from the country, I had never experienced anything like this. I had never been shaken down before.

"If your friends come at me, I will catch you every time

you are alone and rip you apart. Do you hear me?" I asked.

Just then, the teacher came in and we all hurriedly took our seats. The rest of the day, as I went to my classes, I kept my eyes peeled on him and his friends. I tried to be extra careful as I rounded corners or went to the bathroom. I didn't want them to be able to sneak up on me.

Later that day, when it was time for Phys-Ed, we all went to the gym. Our Phys-Ed instructor was a real tall guy. I think I heard someone say he was 6'8". We were instructed to all sit down and then he asked us what we would like to do for Phys-ed.

The kid that had tried to shake me down pointed to me and said, "We want to teach the new kid how to play WAR."

For some reason, the teacher said, "Sure that sounds good."

We were divided up into teams; shirts and skins. When the teacher blew the whistle, everyone started fighting each other to pull the other team off the basketball court. The kid and his friends were left untouched because everyone was afraid of them.

Then, they came at me. They were punching, kicking and grabbing me before I knew what was happening. Somehow, I was able to get into a good position with the biggest guy and I pushed him over the line and off the basketball court. The other two guys were wrestling around, trying to get me across the line, but I slipped between them and got the other big guy over the line. All that was left on the court was me and the big mouth kid who had started all the trouble.

He was in shock and punched me as quick as he could to try to get the upper hand. Well, when he hit me, I hit him as hard as I could. While he was moving backwards to get away from me, I tripped him, grabbed his arm and one leg and sort of slid him over the line. I had won the WAR battle fair and square, but the teacher started yelling at me. He was shouting that I had cheated and the other kid had won. We were the last two on the court and I knew I had won.

The teacher made me run bleacher laps because he said I had cheated. I thought it was odd that he had taken the side of the bully, but I later found out that the Phys-Ed teacher was dating that kid's older sister. Turns out that kid's dad was some kind of big shot in the area and he got by with pretty much anything.

I knew right then and there that the teachers or the principal were not going to help me if I had a problem. I was on my own. I had no friends or anyone that I could count on to back me up. My time at this school was terrible. I tried to make the best of it, but there was just no way.

I generally had to fight the kid and his friends at least once a week. You would think they would eventually give up, but I guess it was a *pride* thing.

The school was so different. I had never been around people who liked people of the same sex. They were called homosexuals. It was so different. There were quite a few of the girls that were already having sex with older guys. I just found the whole thing very strange. It was a rough time in my life. I guess I was just a simple country boy.

Every morning we got up, milked cows, fed the livestock and by the time we were done, we had to catch the bus. We ended up running the half mile lane to catch the bus almost every morning. If we missed the bus, which we did often, we had to run three miles into town to the school.

At least once or twice a week the bus driver would stop at the end of the long lane. He would look right at us and see that we were coming down the lane as fast as we could. He would smirk, shut the door and drive away. We had no doubt he did it just to make us run into town. It seemed as though the whole community was against us.

Later, we would discover that the smart mouth kid's dad was making life tougher for us. I managed to get through that semester, which was the last semester before summer break. I don't think I have ever been as glad to see summer come!

The Cows

School was out and summer was upon us. As usual, we spent our days working on the farm and taking care of the livestock. The number of pigs had increased significantly. We, now, had forty sows and once they all started having litters of little piglets, before we knew it we had almost four-hundred pigs.

We let the cows into the back pasture during the day after the morning milking. They would generally stay back there all day. Sometimes, they liked being out in the pasture so much, they wouldn't come up in the evening. Kenny and I would have to walk all the way back into the pasture to get them. We would drive them up to the barn so we could do our evening milking. It was about a mile back to the back pasture so we were not happy when they didn't come when called. We started heading back there a little early so we could mess around and do some exploring in the woods. The woods had a creek that ran through it.

As it warmed up outside, we would jump over the fence and head into the woods. We would wade around in the creek, catch frogs and crawdads, and cool off for a few minutes. Then, we would round the cows up and drive them home to start milking.

Dad always warned us to be careful around the big Hereford bull that they had in the back pasture. Dad said the bull probably would weigh close to two-thousand pounds. He should have known that was the wrong thing to say to two adventurous boys. We were used to being around animals and had never met one we couldn't make friends with.

On our trips to the back pasture, we started taking some ears of corn with us. We would make sure and give the bull a little bit of the corn at a time until he would follow us around like a puppy dog, a two-thousand pound puppy dog. He started letting us pet him. Then one day, we jumped up on his back. He didn't seem to mind. He headed to the barn with us and the cows would follow. And we didn't have to walk. By the second week of summer, we would go back to get the cows jump up on Herman's back and ride him to the barn. What a perfect way to get the cows herded to the barn.

At the new place, there was a railroad track right out front. We would hear the trains come through every day and at night. It was very noisy. Often, the trains would need to pull over and wait for other trains that were also coming via those tracks to come through. We would see hobo's jump off the trains. Often, they would come up to house begging for food. Mom felt bad for them and would give them some biscuits and a glass of milk. We had to be careful because they would try to sneak in and sleep in the barns. Many of the hobos were drunks and they would smoke cigarettes in the barn. Dad would have to run them off because they didn't want to leave. Sometimes, the running off took place at the end of a rifle.

That same summer, Dad made friends with an old guy named Marvin. Marvin lived down the tracks in an old garage. He and my dad would drink together. Dad would take him to town so he could buy a bottle of booze and some beer. I never did understand why Marvin didn't drive but he didn't. I wonder now if he had his license taken away because of the drinking. So, since Dad was helping drive to get the booze, he also helped him drink his booze.

****

Later that summer, a kid that was my age moved into a house just down from the farm. He came around one day and saw Kenny and I outside doing our chores. He was riding a nice, new, ten speed bike. I mean it was really nice. He was friendly enough, so we talked a while.

Before he left, he said, "Why don't you guys come over and check out our place sometime?"

"Nah, we can't. We have chores to do," we said.

"What, you mean you guys have to work all the time?" he asked.

"Yep," we replied.

We found out the kid's name was Dave and he was in my grade. He was to become a good friend, the only one that I made at that place. Dave stood around and watched us work for the rest of the day. Sometimes, he went back with us to get the cows to bring them up to milk. When he saw us jump up on the bull's back, he loved it!

"Wow! You guys ride that big cow?" he asked.

We laughed and said, "This is not a cow, Dave. This is a bull."

Dave watched us do all our chores that day. He even watched us milk the cows. We were having a great time. Then, Dad came into the barn and saw Dave there. He was not happy that we had someone following us around while we were supposed to be working.

"Boy, I don't need somebody taking these kids away from their work,"

"You go home. You hear me?" Dad told him.

Dave went home just as Dad had instructed, but, the next day I was out in the field running the tractor. Up rides Dave on his ten-speed, right out into the field.

"Hey, can I climb up there and ride that tractor with you?" Dave asked.

"Sure, climb up." I said and I let him get on the tractor. "You sit here and hang on to that fender."

We had a great time. Dave rode with me and we talked for most of the afternoon. The next day, Dave showed up again. This time, he had his dad with him. His dad introduced himself to my dad and we overheard them talking.

"I'm wondering if my boy, Dave, can work with your sons. I think it would be good for him," Dave's dad asked.

"I'm not sure if that would be a good idea. I can't afford to pay the boy," Dad said.

"Dave doesn't need to be paid. The experience would be good for him."

They talked a while longer and finally, Dad agreed that Dave would start working with us boys.

Dave was a big kid. Even though he was only about six

months older than me, he had gone through a growth spurt and was about 5'9". I was only 5"3" at the time. I was twelve and Dave was thirteen at the time. We became fast friends!

We're In the Money!

Dad was plowing a field across the highway. I needed to speak with him, so I had to go across the road and wait until he came around my way with the tractor to talk to him. I was waiting and I saw something odd in the dirt. It looked like an old piece of cloth. When I pulled it out of the dirt and looked at it a little closer, I saw that it was actually a small cloth sack. It was heavier than it looked. I lifted it up out of the dirt completely and coins started dropping out of it. There were about nine or ten coins. I could tell that they were old and they had obviously been buried there for a quite a while. I turned them over and looked at them closely. They were all foreign coins. I figured they were either French or some sort of European coins. The date on one of them was 1828. Wow!

As I was searching through the plowed dirt to see if there were any more bags of coins, Dad pulled up.

"What are you doing, son?"

I held up the bag and the coins in my hand and showed him what I had found. He looked at them closely and suddenly, I saw this gleam come into his eye. He grabbed the coins from me and hurriedly put them in his pocket. He looked around to make sure that no one had seen us. We were close to the highway with traffic coming and going.

"Don't let anyone know about these, you hear me?" He nervously pretended to work on the tractor. "You don't see that old man do you?"

"No," I said after I had looked around.

"Run over and get a stick out of the ditch."

I did as I was told. I ran over and picked one up; I took it back to him. He broke it off over his knee, so it was only about eighteen inches long.

"Now, show me where you found that sack at."

I pointed to the place and he stuck the stick in the ground. He left about six inches sticking out above the ground to mark the spot.

"You make sure not to say anything to anybody about this. Now get back to work."

"But Dad, aren't you going to check out the coins?"

"Not right now. There are too many people going by. Now get back to work, like I said."

The rest of the afternoon I kept thinking *maybe those coins were pirate treasure. Maybe they belonged to a French trapper and he had buried his treasure here. Or maybe, just maybe, the Indians had attacked some settlers and the coins fell out of their wagon.*

Whatever happened, I wanted to get back over there and search for more. But, when Dad told me to do something, I knew that I had to listen or there would be a beating like I had never seen before. So, I worked. I thought the workday was never going to end.

Kenny and I went back as usual and brought the cows up from the pasture. They were taking their time. Even Herman seemed to be walking slower than usual. Sitting on his back, I tried my best to get him to speed up, but he just took his time. Next, we had to milk the cows and get the rest of our chores done. Finally, we were finished.

I went flying into the house. Dad was already there and Mom was getting supper on the table. I didn't say a word, but I could tell Dad was anxious to tell Mom.

"We need to wait until the sun goes completely down," Dad whispered to me.

Finally, after what seemed like forever, the sun went down. Dad stepped over to the back door and looked out. He looked all around the yard. Then, he went into the living room and made sure no one was in the front yard. Mom looked at him oddly.

When he sat down, he told Mom and everyone to be really quiet. "You little ones go into the living room and watch television. I need to talk to your mom."

When he was sure that only he and Mom, Kenny and I were in the kitchen, he pulled the bag out of his pocket. He slowly untied the strings. Once the mouth of the bag was opened, he turned the bag upside down and poured the coins out on the kitchen table

Just as I thought, they were all old. I got excited and tried to reach over to grab the one I had seen first. He smacked my hand. He looked all of them over, but he couldn't tell what they said. He handed one to Mom to look at,

"I can't tell what they say," she said.

Finally, Dad let me pick one up. I had learned about other languages and lands in school and I was pretty sure the big one was French because it said five francs. The date on it read 1828. I looked at the others; they were harder to understand. I just knew they had to be worth a fortune. My imagination was going crazy.

"Go get the flashlight," Dad said.

I flew upstairs to get the flashlight. When I got back down the stairs, he said, "Raymond, I want you to go very slowly and quietly and get the spade and the round point shovel out of the shed. Make sure no one sees or hears you, understand?"

"Yeah, I understand."

"Don't use the flashlight. Leave it here with me. When you get the shovels, meet me out front where nobody can see you in the dusk-to-dawn light."

"Ok, Dad," I said and out the door I went.

I snuck in the shadows to the shed, quietly opened the door and grabbed the shovels. I was careful not to bang them together or make any noise. I closed the shed door and with a shovel in each hand, I snuck around to the front of the house. Dad was out in the front yard waiting on me

"Let's go and no talking."

We didn't go down the lane past the landowner's home. Instead, we went around and climbed over the fence and crossed a pasture. We had to climb over another fence. Then, we crossed the railroad siding and the train tracks. We hid in the ditch whenever traffic went by. Then, we scurried across the highway out and along the field until we thought we were close to the spot where the stick was. We crouched down and between passing cars, Dad would shine the flashlight looking for that stick. We didn't see it!

"Raymond, get down low on the ground. I'll shine the light all around and you look for the stick."

So, I crouched down.

"Kenny, you watch and let us know if a car is coming."

If there was a car coming, the flashlight went out immediately and we all dropped to the ground. It was quite an adventure!

Finally, I spotted that stick we hurried out in the field.

"Dad, there it is!" I whispered, excitedly.

Dad shut off the flashlight and we walked out to the stick. We all started digging.

"If you boys hit anything that sounds like metal or feels like cloth, you stop immediately."

We would check that no cars were coming and then shine the light to see what we had found.

Suddenly, I hit something that clanged a little bit.

"Dad, I hit something."

We looked around to see that no cars were coming, so Dad shined the light. It was just some rocks. Dad turned the light out and we started digging again. Kenny was pulling dirt back with his hands. My mind was racing. We dug down probably three feet and had a hole about three feet around. We found nothing, absolutely nothing! We were all pretty disappointed.

"Raymond, go get some more sticks."

It was getting late and we had milking to do in the morning. Dad had us fill the hole in and then placed the sticks at the mouth of dig site.

"Okay, be quiet about this and we will come back out tomorrow night and try again."

Back to the road we went, trying to cover our tracks as we went. We went back down in the ditch and hid until no traffic was coming, then we ran across the road, over the tracks, back across the pasture and snuck into the house. We brought the dirty shovels right into the house with us.

"Get cleaned up and get to bed."

So, Kenny and I went upstairs and washed up. We got into bed, but there wasn't any sleeping gonna happen tonight. My mind was still thinking of buried treasure. It was exciting, yet it was torture. I knew we had to work all day and that treasure was just waiting for us to dig it up.

I could hear Mom and Dad talking downstairs. They were talking about buying our own farm, but they said we had to be careful. "We have to be careful because we found the money on the owners' land. They could lay claim to it." Dad was as excited as we were and they weren't sleeping either.

Kenny started asking me all sorts of questions about what we would do with the money. We talked about buying a motorcycle. We didn't realize how tired we were, and we finally drifted off to sleep.

When the next morning arrived, so did Dave. He was banging on the door downstairs. We had all overslept, even Dad. The cows were bellowing, wanting to be milked so we grabbed our clothes and ran out the door without breakfast. We just ran out to the barn, brought the cows in for milking and that's how our day started.

All day, the chores dragged on and on. Dave helped as much as he could, but it was his first day. I was so tired, I kept yawning over and over.

"How come you are so tired," Dave asked.

"I didn't sleep too well. None of us did."

The time arrived for us to head back and bring the cows up for the evening milking. We took off as usual, walking through the pasture and then back to the little creek. We decided we needed a swim. We stripped off our clothes and waded in. It felt great. We were only in about eighteen inches to two feet of water, so we laid back and let the water flow over us. I was so exhausted, I could have gone to sleep right there in that water, but I was daydreaming about spending that money.

Suddenly, I realized that we had to get the milking done. We needed to head back up to the house, so Dave could head home and we could get back to the dig site. So, Kenny and I hurried Dave out of the water.

"Come on, Dave, we don't want to get in trouble."

Dave hurriedly put his clothes back on and we climbed on Herman's back. We led the cows up and after milking, we said goodbye to Dave. He wasn't in much of a hurry, but we finally persuaded him to leave.

We completed our chores and headed into the house for supper. By the time Kenny and I got in the house, Dad was talking with Mom.

"You know, if there is anything else out there, we have to find it tonight, because the old man wants that field disked and planted before the weather changes."

He also mentioned that it was supposed to rain the next several days and we would need to get the field ready to plant. The soybeans had to be put in the ground, so they could start the growing process.

During dinner, we were all thinking about what we needed to do and that we needed to do it quickly. After supper, Dad sent the young ones into the living room to watch TV. We sat and talked about our situation, very quietly of course.

"I figure I was plowing about nine to ten inches deep when I hit that bag of coins. The tractor was going about three miles an hour so I probably drug that bag about two or three feet before it rolled up on top of the ground. I think we were digging about three feet too far into the field. Tonight is the last time we will be able to dig, so we have to work at it really hard. We need to find the spot and dig about two to three feet back from where we were last night," Dad said.

We all agreed and a plan was formulated. We each knew just what we had to do. So, we waited until after 9 o'clock. Once the sun went down, we snuck out the front door and back out into the field. Once again, I found myself laying in the ditch with Dad shining the light across the field to find the sticks. We were again waiting on cars to go by, then jumping up again and digging like crazy. We dug and dug and never found anything.

"Well boys, if it's out here, it must be over this way."

He pointed to the east side of where we had been digging.

"We didn't figure in the fact that the dirt was thrown over from one spot to the other. It's late, so let's get out of here. I will see if I can put the old man off tomorrow, so we have one more night to dig. If we don't find anything then, well, then that's it."

I was devastated, but I knew he was right. As we lay in

bed that night, Kenny and I talked and talked about those coins. We talked most of the night. We just knew that there was a treasure trove just waiting for us out in that field.

That next morning, Dave had to wake us up, again. He was pounding on the back door like a madman. We had overslept again and we were even more exhausted than the day before. We started milking the cows and man, were they mad at us because we were late. You know, animals have tempers, too, and they let you know when they are not happy. They can be temperamental, too. There were certain cows that wanted me to milk them and certain cows that only wanted Kenny to milk them. I'm not sure what it was, but they had their preferences and they did not like change.

We finished milking and were putting the milk in the milk house when I heard a tractor running. It sounded like it was on the property across the road. I went out of the milk house and could not believe my eyes. Out there in the field was the old guy who owned the house. He was disking. He had been out there for over an hour and we hadn't even realized it. He had completely disked up the ground we had been digging in.

My heart was racing! What to do? I ran down the lane and crossed the road as quickly as I could. When he finally came around close to me with the tractor, I yelled up at him.

"We were planning on disking that field later."

"Oh, I know. I just thought I would help get a jump on it for you."

While we were talking, I was scanning the area to see if the sticks that we had left to mark our spot were still there. They were gone! The whole place had been disked and it all just looked the same. I was crushed because I knew our treasure hunt was over.

I didn't say a word to the old man and we all kept it very quiet. At least we had the original bag of coins we had found. We needed to see how much they were worth. As soon as we could get into town, we stopped into a little coin shop. It wasn't in a good part of town, but Dad took the coins in to see what they were worth. The guy said he would give Dad twenty bucks for them. I was shocked! Only twenty bucks! And for a second I thought Dad was going to take it. Thank goodness he didn't and the coins came back home with us. Dad put the coins away in a safe place and life went on. I thought they should be worth at least a few hundred dollars. Come to think of it I never saw those coins again. I still don't know, to this day, what happened to them or what they may have been worth.

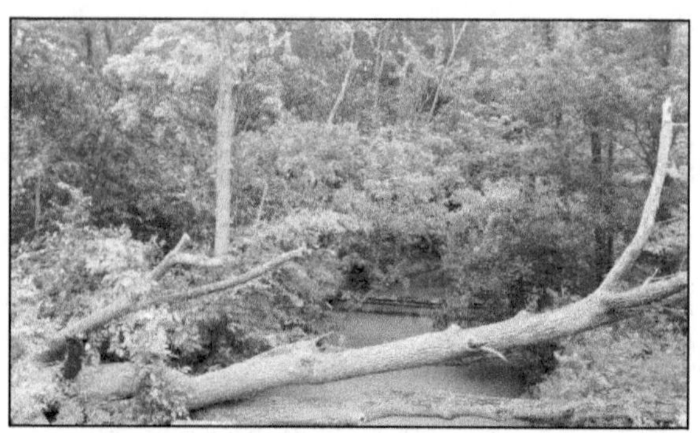

The Creek and Learning to Swim

It was summer once again. We started heading back to get the cows as early as we could so we could have some play time in the creek. We would hurry through our chores then, Kenny, Dave and I would go back to the creek. We caught frogs, crawdads and waded in the creek. We worked hard and this was our fun time.

One day, we were exploring and walked up the creek a little further than we had before. I was in the lead and walking in water less than a foot deep. The water was murky and I couldn't see the bottom, but I assumed it had been like it always had been, less than knee deep.

All of a sudden, I stepped forward and the creek bottom was gone. Before I knew it, I was sinking down, down, down.

I didn't know how to swim and neither did my brother or Dave, for that matter. I started kicking and splashing. I was running out of air and the surface wasn't in sight. I kicked even harder until I reached the top. I was able to grab a breath of air and then down I went again. Once again, I kicked and splashed my way up and made my way over to the shore. Finally, my foot hit the bottom and I lunged on to the shore, exhausted. We were all scared, but no one as much as me. That was the end of wading for that day. Once I caught my breath, we went up got the cows and rode Herman to the barn.

The next day we went back to the creek and the water was clear. We weren't going to give up playing in the creek, but we went a lot more cautiously. We waded back to where I had stepped into the hole. There was a huge rock there under the water. Since it was clearer today, we could see that it was all washed out in front of the rock. It formed a nice wide spot, probably about twenty foot by thirty or thirty-five foot long.

We grabbed some sticks and started probing the bottom to see how deep it was. I would guess now, it was about seven foot in the deepest part. We discovered that it actually angled up with a sandy bottom. That sandy edge made it perfect for us to come into it from the upstream side and play around without being in any danger. We had our own private swimming hole! Even though none of us could swim at the time. Little-by-little, we taught ourselves how to swim. We would go every day possible and swim a little while.

We were swimming one day when a couple of kids from the houses on the road north of the farm came back to explore. They were city kids and were really shocked to see that people actually swam in the creek. One kid named Ricky, seemed like an okay kid. He wanted to swim with us, so we invited him in. We swam and played around catching crawdads for a good while.

Then, like we always did when we were done swimming, we got out on the bank and started checking ourselves for leeches.

"What are you guys doing?" Ricky asked.

Just then, he saw something on his belly. He tried to brush it off, but it wouldn't come off.

"This leaf is stuck on me."

I was smoking at the time and I had just lit a cigarette. I turned to look and said, "That's not a leaf. That's a leech."

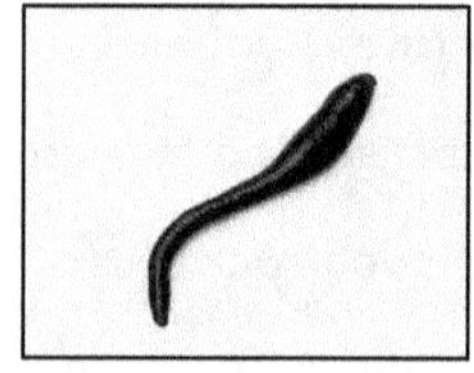

"What is a leech?"

Laughing, I said, "You mean to tell me, you don't know what a leech is?"

"No, what is it?"

"A leech is a little animal that lives in the water. They latch on to other animals and suck their blood."

Ricky went wild! He kept repeatedly trying to wipe it off of his belly and it just wouldn't come loose. He finally started crying and screaming.

"Get it off! Get it off!"

I casually reached over and took the cigarette out of my mouth. I touched the leech with the lit end and it curled up and fell off. It left a little trail of Ricky's blood on his stomach.

"Oh, NO! I'm bleeding."

He was so upset, I thought he was going to pass out. Then, a look of relief came over his face.

"Man, I'm glad I got that thing off me."

"Well, you better check to see if there are any more on you."

He screamed! "WHAT! You mean that there might be more of them?"

"Well, you have to check."

Ricky looked all over his legs, arms and his belly. Then he had Kenny look at his back.

"Whew, no more leeches. That had me scared to death."

"You still have to take your shorts off and look because those guys can get anywhere."

Kenny and I had already changed out of our shorts and checked ourselves. We were good. Ricky pulled the waist of his shorts back very, very slowly. We could tell he was terrified to look. He finally mustered up the courage and looked into his shorts. He instantly let out this God-Awful sound. It sounded like he was dying. Tears were running down his cheeks and he was breathing so fast we thought his chest would explode.

"Oh! NOOOOO! I have one on my dick. What do I do?"

By this time all three of us, Kenny, myself and Ricky's friend, were laughing so hard we were crying, too, but not from fear. I took the cigarette I was smoking and handed it to him.

"Here, you use it and keep it," I said.

"What do I do with it?

"Touch the leech with it and it will drop off."

Ricky dropped his shorts down around his ankles and started to touch the leech, but it moved. He let out another big scream.

"What happens if I leave it there?"

"Well, it will eat its way into your blood stream and just keep drinking your blood."

He was shaking. He started to touch the cigarette to the leech again and it moved.

"Here, one of you guys do it."

"No way," we all said in unison. "You are on your own."

Finally, he touched the leech with the cigarette and it dropped off. He sat down on a log and continued sobbing. At least now, he was relieved that it was gone.

I couldn't resist. "You better check the rest of yourself to see if there are any more."

He got up and started looking at his private area and all over his body. As he turned around away from us, there was the biggest leech I had ever seen hanging on his right butt cheek. We had all seen it at the same time; all except Ricky, of course. We started laughing so hard we were literally rolling on the ground.

"What? What? Don't tell me there are more." You could hear the fear in his voice.

Through our laughter, Kenny finally said, "Yeah, there is and this one is huge."

Dave reached out with a cigarette, touched the leech and it dropped off. Needless to say, Ricky never got in the swimming hole again. He would come over and watch us swim, but he never got back in the water.

One day, on our way back to our swimming hole, we were walking down by the creek and we heard voices and some laughing. We snuck down closer and followed the sound of the voices. They were coming from a little bluff near the creek. We climbed up so we could see who it was.

There was a man and woman spooning. If you don't know what spooning is, it is …well I'll let you figure it out. They started taking off their clothes. *Hmmm, interesting!*

We sat down on the bluff and watched, as they got lost in what they were doing. Suddenly, a voice yelled from the edge of the woods and broke our concentration. It was our little brother, Darrel, he had followed us back and had gotten lost.

The couple raised up, then must have decided the voice was so far away there was no reason for alarm. We continued to watch them and when they finished they were smoking a cigarette.

"I don't want my husband to find out about this," the woman said.

Suddenly, we understood. She was cheating and that was why they were hiding in the woods. We were ornery kids and didn't like the fact that she was cheating on her husband. So, we reached up while they were talking and stole their clothes. We took off with their clothes and dropped them down by the creek. Then, we headed out of the woods. We heard the man shouting.

"Hey, you kids bring back those clothes."

We grabbed Darrel and ran as quick as we could over to get the cows. We were laughing hysterically. But, honestly, I was glad to jump up on Herman's back. I knew that even as mad as that guy was, he wouldn't dare take on that big bull at least not naked.

The Old German Lady

One day, while I was out working, the old German lady who owned the farm, came out to the barn, and asked me if I would help her get her flower beds cleaned up.

"Young man, would you help me clean out and plant my flower beds? I will be happy to pay you for your help."

"Yes," I said, "as long as my dad says it is okay."

She asked Dad and he agreed. I don't think he felt like he had much choice since she owned the farm. I went over to her big house and she started showing me the enormity of the project I had taken on. She had flower beds all around the house and she didn't just want me to clean and help plant the flower beds, she wanted me to do major landscaping. I began to clean and cut out shrubs by hand; I worked for hours that first day. She wasn't helping, but she stood over me the whole time. She pushed me hard, and I had stepped right into being her slave.

I worked for her for days. As soon as the milking was done in the morning, I would go over to her house and start working on those flower beds and shrubbery. What I didn't know was that she was having friends come over and wanted the place looking like her mansion. It was a big old farmhouse and it was nice, but a mansion it was not.

After ten days of back-breaking work, it was time for me to get paid. I had worked at least a hundred hours on the flower and shrubbery. I was expecting a big reward. The old woman had me come into her house. That was very different for her, because she didn't want us in there normally. She told the old man to get me my money I was due. He had me go with him into his 'study', he called it. When we got in there, he pulled a big picture off the wall. There was a safe door built into the wall. I thought it was really neat. He now had my attention.

"Turn your back, son."

I did as he asked.

He spun the combination around and I heard the door click open.

"Alright, you can turn around now."

When I turned around, I saw bundles of money in the safe, more money than I had ever seen in my life. He pulled out an envelope with some cash in it and looked through it until he found what he wanted; pulled out a bill and handed it to me. It was a five dollar bill. As I looked at that five dollars I thought about how hard I had worked and for all those hours.

"Is this all I get?"

"That's five dollars."

I stormed out of that house with a sense of disbelief and just plain anger. That was the first time I felt like I had just been taken advantage of. BIG TIME taken advantage of.

When I got to our house, I threw the door open. Mom was standing there and could see I was upset.

"Raymond, what's the matter?"

When I told her what had happened, I saw the Irish fire rise up in her face. My mom knew how hard and how long I had worked making that old lady's place look like a show place.

"Well, maybe they just didn't pay you all of it."

"No, they had plenty of money. They just took advantage of me," I said.

"Well, don't worry," she said, "It will all work out."

"I think I need to just tell them off."

"No, you can't do that. They are the landowners and they could order us off the place. Then what would we do?"

I stormed out to help Kenny milk the cows and put the milk in the cooler.

That evening, when Dad came in, he said, "Did the old lady pay you today? How much did you make for helping her?"

I didn't want to say because I knew it would cause trouble. Mom beat me to it.

"That old tight wad only gave him five dollars for all the

work he did."

"What! Five dollars! That's not enough for all that work."

I could see he was mad and disappointed because they were hoping to take the money from me to help buy groceries.

"Hmmmm, we will have to do something else," Dad said.

The next several days, every time I saw them, I looked at that old couple with disgust. Whenever I saw them, I felt anger boil up inside me. I finally started avoiding looking at them because I didn't like feeing that way. They didn't talk to me because I stayed away. I kept myself busy working with the livestock or out in the fields. The days rolled by and I was doing better with my anger. But, I was still bitter about the way they had treated me.

The Bull

One afternoon we were riding the bull back to bring the cows up from the pasture. As we walked under an old apple tree, Dave reached up and picked a green apple. It looked pretty good, so I picked one for me and one for Kenny. They were just out of his reach. Heck, I even picked one for Herman the bull. All of a sudden, we heard this awful shrieking voice yelling at us. It was the old German woman.

"Get down off that bull and stop stealing my apples."

We jumped down off the bull and went on up to the barn, but it was too late. We looked over and she had Dad cornered out by the barn screaming at the top of her lungs.

"Those boys were riding that bull and stealing my apples."

Oh, crap. I thought. We knew we were in for it. Dad was glaring at us.

"I will take care of it," Dad said.

He grabbed me by the upper arm and made a big show of taking me to the barn.

"Kenny, you follow me. Dave, you get your butt home."

All the while he was pulling me into the barn, I thought for sure he was going to break my arm. Once inside, he cussed such a stream of profanity I couldn't even understand it. I knew it was going to be a beating I wouldn't forget.

As he was pulling his belt out of his pants he said, "How long have you boys been riding that bull?"

"All summer, Dad."

"I told you that big bull was dangerous and to not be around him."

"Yeah, we know, but we had already made friends with him before that and he is a big gentle bull. He follows us all over the pasture. We jump up on him and the cows follow him in every night."

Dad took the belt he was swinging and started hitting the burlap feed bags beside him as if he was spanking me. Then, he grabbed Kenny and he yelled and cussed some more. Then, oddly, he started hitting the feed bags again.

"Now go get those cows milked and don't you let me find out that you been doing anything like that again."

We stood there in shock!

"I said get those cows milked!"

We ran over and started to milk the cows. On our way, we saw the old lady standing out beside the barn. She had been listening the whole time. She had a look of satisfaction on her face.

At supper that night, Dad told Mom what had happened. She was steamed, I could tell. Mom was always a peaceful sort of woman. She was loving and kind, but if someone were to come against her kids that Irish temper of hers would flare up. She was like a mama bear protecting her cubs. You didn't want her to get going.

Two days later, I came in for lunch from working out in the field. Mom was in the kitchen.

"I noticed that the blackberries over by the fence are ripe, will you go over and pick them for me?" she asked. "I will make us a blackberry cobbler tonight."

That was all that needed to be said. I was headed out the door and on my way. Blackberry cobbler was and still is my favorite. I was happily picking those blackberries and all of a sudden there was that loud unforgettable voice screaming at me that I was stealing the blackberries. It was the old German woman again. She was just giving me a tongue-lashing.

"If you want the blackberries, you can have those too," I said. "You already have everything else."

I just let go; ranting and raving.

"You are the greediest person I have ever met. You cheated me out of my pay and I worked really hard to help you."

She grabbed the bucket of blackberries I had picked and took off to her house muttering and mumbling as she went. I walked back over to our house, feeling defeated and angry again.

"Did you get them picked?"

"Yep, I did, but the old woman came out and jumped all over me and I told her to take the blackberries along with everything else she has."

"She took those blackberries from you after you picked them?"

"Yes, Mom, she did."

Mom practically tore off her apron and threw it on the floor. There was fire in her eyes like I had never seen before. She stormed out of the house and headed across the barn yard. I watched as she went right in that old ladies back door and started yelling at her. The old woman mouthed off and mom pushed her up against her kitchen stove and let her have it. She told her absolutely everything that was on her mind.

My mom was only 5 foot 3 inches and maybe weighed 135 pounds. The old woman was probably five foot eight inches and was well over 300 pounds. She could tell how mad

Mom was and she didn't dare take her on. I watched through the back door as Mom reached over and picked up that bucket of blackberries. She turned them upside down and dumped them all over the old woman's sparkling white kitchen range. Then, she smashed them into the white porcelain on that range.

"I expect you to pay my son for the work he did for you on your flower beds or I'm going to turn you into the child labor people."

Mom stormed out of the house. She grabbed me by the arm as she came through the door. My jaw must have been wide open.

"Don't look at me like that," she said.

All the way back to the house I said "Wow, Mom, I never saw you like that before."

She didn't say anything. When we got inside the house she told me to get back to work. As I was leaving the house, I could hear her crying in the living room.

The next day, the old woman called my little brother Darrel out of the yard and handed him an envelope. It was addressed to me and it had forty dollars in it. I never thanked them. They didn't deserve a thank you.

Football Practice

I knew that football practice was about to start and Dave and I had been talking about it for weeks. I talked and talked to Dad about it because I really wanted to play.

"Dad, please I really want to play football."

"Well the planting is all done, I guess if you make your own way to practice you can go for a couple of hours once in a while."

Each day, after I got my chores done, I ran the three and a half miles to school and usually got there just as practice was starting. That first day when I arrived and headed out onto the field, who did I see but that big, tall Phys-Ed teacher. He was the coach.

"What are you doing here?"

"I want to play football."

He took one look at me and said, "You're too small to play football. What position do you think you could play?"

"I could play quarterback or maybe a running back."

He smirked and said, "We have our quarterback."

He pointed at that big mouth kid that I'd had problems with for two semesters.

"Well, I can be a running back."

"You're too small."

I looked around and pointed right at his quarterback. "He's no bigger than I am." Well, he wasn't any taller, but he was at least thirty pounds heavier than I was.

A bunch of the other kids said, "Let the little kid play, coach."

I'm guessing there was enough of a group encouraging him, so he said, "Well, let's just see if you can make it or not."

He called the defense up had them get set. He had the quarterback hand me the ball and then try to make it through the defensive line. I wasn't big, but I was strong. All that cow milking, putting up hay and working on the farm everyday paid off. I straight-armed a couple those big guys and squirmed through the blockade.

The coach was really ticked off. He made us run the play again. I don't know how I managed. I guess it just seemed to come natural to me this time. I broke through again and ran the ball about twenty yards and put it down in the end zone. He still didn't like it, but the coach could see that I had potential.

Every school day, I would work all morning, run the three and a half miles to school to practice and then run back home to milk the cows. The coach made it rough on me though because he just didn't like me. He made my practices harder than anyone else and intentionally tried to get me to quit. He was constantly berating me and trying to embarrass me in front of the team. He picked on me about my clothes, but when it came my turn to carry the ball something would happen and I was unstoppable. I don't know what it was, maybe it was fear? I sure didn't want those bigger guys hitting me. Somehow, I dodged them completely or they would just get a glancing shot on me.

Summer Break is Too Short

Finally, summer arrived again. I hated school so I was glad to see it come. My summer days were very full of doing all my chores on the farm and running to and from practice.

Before I knew it, it was time for school to start again. I hated the thought of going back to school. It was the worst for me. Then, I thought, *well, at least I have our first football game that first week of school.*

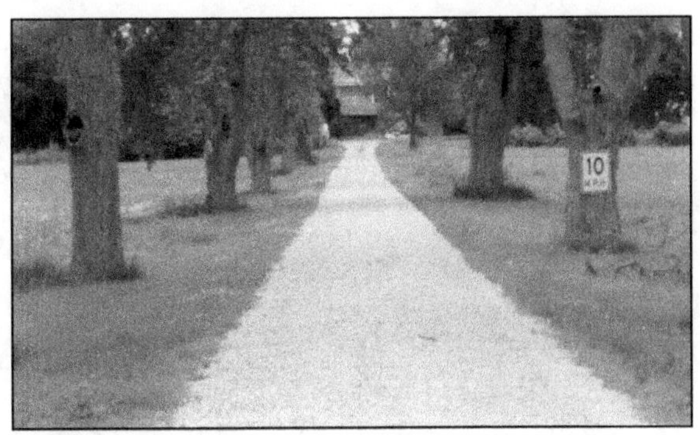

After Kenny and I got the cows milked, we headed down the lane to catch the bus. The bus driver pulled up just as we were about halfway, so we picked up our little brothers and sister and ran. He intentionally pulled away, laughing at us as he shut the door.

We finally made it to school that first day. I started trying to find my classes. Unfortunately, I walked into my second class and the big-mouthed quarterback was there. He came over with his friends. His friends weren't eligible to play football because they couldn't keep their grades up.

The quarterback came up to me and said, "Just to let you know, this year is not going to be like last year. I have some help and you are going to do what I say. Oh and you are not going to play football on my team."

I ignored him, shrugged it off and went on with my classes the rest of the day. I can't say the rest of that day was spectacular, but it was so-so.

The next day, we had Phys-Ed. In walks the coach. He started all the football players doing bleacher runs and things seemed okay. When I went into the showers after we were done, I was washing quickly and trying to get out of there. Out of the blue, a big kid reached over and grabbed me by my penis. I had been told he was homosexual, but didn't believe it until that moment. Something in me snapped. I punched him in the jaw. I hit him hard and he fell back and cracked his head on the tile surrounding the shower. It made a big gash in his scalp and he noticed he was bleeding. I ignored him and walked over and started getting dressed. After all, it was his fault he should have never grabbed me.

The coach came in. "What did you do that for?"

I was trying to explain to him what happened and as I was finishing the first part of my sentence he back handed me as hard as he could across the face. It knocked me against the lockers. He grabbed me by the arm and took me to the office.

When we got to the office, the principal and all of the staff started calling me trash and other bad names. These were adults and they were even threatening me. They called my mom and told her to come and get me.

I waited what seemed like forever. Finally, when Mom came in, Dad was with her. The principal and teachers wouldn't let me speak to Mom and Dad at first. They told my parents that I had assaulted another student and that he had to be taken to the hospital.

Dad walked around the corner where I was sitting.

"Did that kid hit you as hard as you hit him?" he asked.

"No, he didn't hit me at all. He grabbed my penis and I hit him."

"What happened to your face then?"

"The Phys-Ed coach backhanded me across the face."

It was as though a bomb went off in the room. My dad exploded. Dad looked at that coach with fire in his eyes. The coach raised up from where he was sitting and stood up in front of Dad. He towered over my dad. But, my dad looked even bigger than he usually did. I swear he looked like he was 6'10" to me at that moment.

"You hit my son?"

"Yeah I did, and if you want to make anything of it I will kick your ass, too."

Whew, that was the wrong thing to say. My dad hit him so fast and hard in the stomach it looked like his fist was gonna come out the coach's back. The punch immediately doubled him over.

"Now you're not so big are you, you son-of-a-bitch."

Dad hit him two more times and left him lying in the floor of the office, moaning and groaning.

He looked at me and said, "Come on, we're going home."

The principal and all the others were scattering to get out of Dad's way. They were falling over chairs and one another to give us room to leave.

When we got home, I looked in the mirror in the bathroom and was shocked. The whole side of my face was swollen and I had a black eye from where the coach had hit me. When I came out of the bathroom, I could see in Dad and Mom's faces. We were in trouble. They were just waiting for the police to come to get me and now, Dad, too. Me for hitting the kid and Dad for beating up that coach.

"I'm sorry, Dad. That kid grabbed me there and I just hit him. It was instinct."

"Don't worry about it. I would have done the same

thing."

I knew my dad. I knew he was thinking that he was going to be arrested for beating up the coach. I was scared, too, but it didn't happen. The coach had hit a thirteen-year-old kid. I found out later that he would have been the one going to jail, so no one ever pressed any charges. The police never came, but with all the worry and pain in my cheek, it was a rough night. That was the last time I went to that school. So, the quarterback was right, I didn't get to play football that year.

Dave's Family Moves

The next day, as soon as we got done milking, I went over to Dave's house to check on him; he hadn't been in school the day before. He hadn't come over to our house, either. When I got over there I could hear the TV playing, but no one was coming to the door. Finally, I looked through the window where there were some curtains that were slightly open. I could see his little brother and sister sitting in the living room watching TV. I pecked on the window and they came over and looked out, when they saw it was me they came to the door. They were good little kids. They were about seven and eight years old.

"We can't let anybody in 'cause Dad and Mom told us not to."

"Oh," I asked. "Where are they?"

"We can't tell you."

"Well, why aren't you guys in school?"

"We are all moving and we are going to go to a new school."

"That's the first I had heard about you guys moving."

"Well, it just happened. We are moving this weekend."

"Where is Dave?"

"Mom and Dad took him to the hospital."

"What? Why?"

The little boy said, "Dave had a bottle stuck on his peepee."

"What?"

"Yeah, he had a milk bottle stuck on his peepee."

At this point I'm laughing hysterically. "You mean down here?" I said and pointed down to my crotch.

"Yeah. Dad was really mad at Dave."

"Okay, well I have to go back to work, but if you guys need anything until your mom and dad get back, you come over."

"Okay, thanks."

Even with my black eye and the big bruise on my face, I couldn't help but laugh as I went back up the lane. That was about the funniest thing I had heard for a long time. It made me forget about the pain for a few minutes.

Later that afternoon, Dave came over. We were out in the barn, milking the cows. I had already told Kenny about Dave's little mishap with the milk bottle. It didn't take long for us to start giving him grief over it.

"Hey, never mind that, what happened to your face?" Dave asked.

I had to tell him the story about the coach hitting me.

"Wow your dad beat the coach up?"

"Yep, he sure did."

"Yeah, we could hear it all the way down to our classroom," Kenny said.

"Hey, why are you guys moving?"

"We are moving so Dad can be closer to his work. We need to get a cheaper place to live."

"When are you moving?" Kenny and I both asked at the same time

"This weekend."

We all hated it because we had become good friends that summer. Little did we know what was going to happen the next day.

Dad Has a Heart Attack

The next day, we were getting ready to do the morning milking. Dad was getting the tractor ready to move some equipment. He took off on the tractor and we turned to go into the milk house. We heard something that sounded kinda funny. It sounded like a thud. I turned around and Dad was laying on the ground. The tractor was moving with no one on it. I ran over, jumped on the tractor, and finally got it stopped. I shut it off and then ran over to check on Dad. He was laying on the ground in the mud and cow manure. He kept trying to sit up, so I helped him. He sat there for a little while.

"Help me get on my feet," he said.

Kenny and I pulled him up to his feet. He was still staggering. I held him up while Kenny ran ahead. Dad leaned on me and we headed toward the house. Mom came flying out of the house when Kenny told her what was going on.

"Help me get him in the car."

We put him in the car and Mom jumped in and took off to the hospital.

We continued working until the little kids got home from school. We took them into the house and helped find them something to eat. Before long, Mom came driving up. Dad wasn't with her.

"Your dad had a heart attack and he's going to be in the hospital for a little while. You and Kenny are going to have to take care of the livestock and the milking until we find out what is going to happen."

It sounded like a lot of work, but we took care of the livestock most of the time anyway. Dad was usually off doing something else. We just wouldn't have Dad telling us what needed to be done each day. We were old enough and had worked on the farm enough that we knew what to do. The big thing was that the crops were about to be ready to harvest. We knew that was something we couldn't handle by ourselves.

Dad came home in a couple of days. When he went to the doctor for his check up at the end of that week, the doctor told him that he'd had a stress related heart attack.

"You need to get away from the farm and that old woman who owns it. It is too much on you."

"How do you know that old woman?"

"She's my aunt. She is the most obstinate human being I've ever been around. I don't know how you have been able to work for her as long as you have. Anyway, your days of farming are over. You aren't going to be able to work for at least six months. Then, we will check you to see how your heart is doing."

We knew that was not good news. Dad had always farmed. What were we going to do now? How and where were we going to live? Everything was up in the air.

The next day, Dad walked over to tell the old German woman what was going on with his health. She was only worried about how the farm would be taken care of.

"My boys and I will take care of the milking. We will split the cows up between us. I will do my best to see that the crops are harvested."

That next week the milk man told Dad and the old lady about someone who would buy the milk cows. We were going to keep our two. It just so happened that they were dry at the time and not producing milk. That worked out to our benefit. We didn't have to milk them.

Kenny and I helped load those milk cows up and as they drove down the lane, I remember saying "So long, Flossy."

Man, was I glad to see those cows leave. A couple of days later, the pigs were sold. My granddad found us a little house and one acre of ground for sale. It was small, but we had to have some place to live. The banker that Dad had borrowed money from for the equipment helped him get the loan to buy the house. He also helped Dad make arrangements to sell all of our equipment. We sold off almost everything that belonged to us from the farm and moved into a new house within a week. We started school at a new school, so I didn't have to go back and face the coach and principal at my old school. I was happy to move away so I didn't have to go back to that school.

My uncles and granddad helped us get the crops in at the old woman's farm on the weekends. As soon as that was done, the equipment was moved to another farm. It was going to be sold at a farm auction.

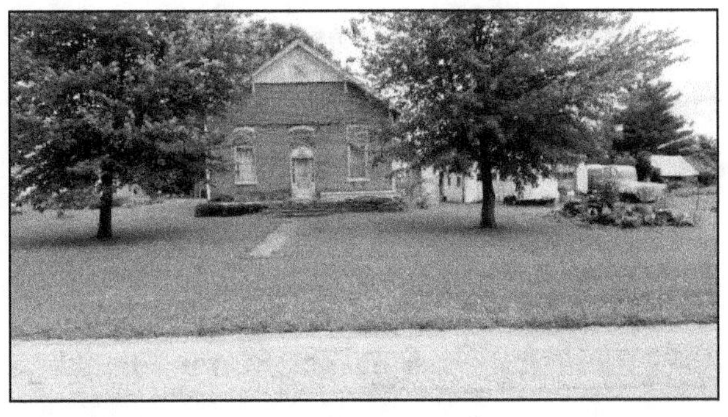

The New Place in Town

There was a quick realization that we had, once again, moved to a different kind of community. Although it appeared to be mostly farms all around us, I was soon to discover that the little town of about 500 people, was very different. It wasn't the regular farm experience of the other places and yet, it was not the suburban area like the place we had just left.

This little town had one stop sign with a red flashing light. There was an old filling station and a little general store. The people that lived there that had kids in our age group were too poor to own farmland. Their dad's worked in town. They were on the lower end of the blue collar scale. Some of them worked construction for a few months a year. When it got cold, they were out of work.

We were probably a sight to see. We came rolling into town with two milk cows, a quarter horse and about twenty piglets. We were all living on a one acre tract in the middle of town. Needless to say, the people in this little town were not too happy to see farm animals.

There was one really rich old guy who lived in town. His family lived near him. There was the retired old man and the woman who lived across the road from us; both thought the animals needed to be somewhere else. We found out that the house we bought was a foreclosure and the family that lost the house was not happy that we had bought the place. They still lived in town and had friends there, so they were constantly stirring up trouble with the people around us.

The New School in Town

My first day of school at the new school was intense. I had to walk up the street to the filling station to catch the bus with all the junior high and High school kids. There were quite a few kids that caught the bus there. The older guys were definitely more of the hoodlum type, not like the farm kids I had known before. These guys were prone to stealing and thieving. They were all older than me, and I was definitely smaller than any of them.

One other kid who caught the bus there ended up being in my class. He was still bigger than I was because he had failed a grade or two. He didn't quite seem right and seemed pretty slow-witted. The bus arrived and we climbed on. Some smart aleck kid told the bus driver that I was new and that he would probably have to babysit me. Oh, no, I couldn't let that go unchallenged!

"Oh yeah," I said loudly, "I would hate to cut in on your babysitting time for him."

A few people laughed, but the kid didn't think it was very funny. He was a really big kid and a bully. He was used to getting his way. He was at least three years older and three times bigger than I was.

I walked down the aisle of the bus and no one wanted to

let the 'new' kid sit with them. I finally got somebody to let me sit with them and rode the 4 miles to school in silence. I went to the office, checked in, got my class schedule and started trying to find my classes. It was chaos. Everyone was running through the halls trying to get to their classes. I had no idea where I was going and no one would stop to help. I saw a teacher and stopped to ask him where I needed to go.

"Excuse me, I'm new, can you point me in the right direction to my first class?"

"Go to the room at the end of the hall."

I made it to that first class and when the bell rang, I started looking for my next class. I was looking around when suddenly, the principal grabbed me by the arm. He pulled me to the side of the hall out of traffic.

"Is your name Stanton?"

"Yes, it is."

"I'm the principal here and I don't want to have any trouble out of you."

"I'm not causing any trouble."

"I heard you cussed out a teacher."

"What! No."

I was in shock. I hadn't even talked to any teachers other than the one I asked for directions to my class.

"I had your brothers in school and you'd better not act

anything like them.”

“You couldn’t have had my brothers. They are all younger than me and they go to elementary school.”

“Then, who is your dad?”

I told him and he said, “Is Mark your Granddad?”

“Yes, he is.”

“Well, I had your uncles in school and if I have any problems with you, I’m going to paddle your butt with a board and ask questions later, do you understand me?

“Yep,” I said, “I understand.”

He let go of my arm and started walking down the hall.

“Hey, I still need to know where my next class is.”

“Find it yourself and you better not come to me for a hall pass for being late.”

The warning bell had already sounded and the hall was empty by the time I found my class. I walked in and the teacher scowled at me.

“Who are you and why are you late?”

“Oh,” I said, “The principal was talking to me in the hall. Turns out he knows my uncles.”

“Oh, okay. Take a seat,” the teacher said.

I sat down with a sigh of relief that he didn’t send me to the office for a hall pass. During class, some of the boys around my desk started whispering to me.

"Hey, new kid, what was the principal talking to you about? We saw him holding your arm; he didn't look happy with you at all."

"No big deal. Somehow he got the idea that I cussed out a teacher."

"Wow! You cussed out a teacher? Is this your first day?"

"Yes, this is my first day and no I didn't cuss out a teacher."

I tried to set them straight, but they only heard what they wanted to hear. They didn't listen to the part where I tried to explain that I hadn't cussed out a teacher. By the end of the day it was all over school that I had cussed out a teacher and the principal had given me a big-time talking to about it.

That night on the bus, the High school kids said, "Here, you can sit with us."

I sat down and they started talking to me like I was their best friend.

"We heard you cussed out a teacher on your first day of school. We heard that Principal Wade grabbed you and pulled you over in the hallway."

"Yeah, it was a misunderstanding. He told me that he was going to bust my butt with a board if I caused any problems."

"Wow! Not bad for your first day, kid."

The older guys were smacking me on the back saying *way*

to go, but the big kid from that morning on the bus wasn't happy. He was a sophomore and he wanted to be 'in' with the older guys. So, I quickly made an enemy.

This school was ok. At least it was better than my last school. My teachers were friendlier, even if I was a farm kid. At least I didn't feel they were judging me. I started making some friends in class and with the older guys on the bus. If I was walking in the hallway and one of the high school kids saw me, they would shout my name and do a little head nod. I think they thought I was a pretty cool kid. I had earned a reputation and I hadn't even done anything.

The guys in my class took notice, so I was suddenly one of the bad boy-cool kids in the school. That big kid saw that I was 'in' with the older guys, so he started asking me to play football with him and his friends in town. We played tackle with no pads or helmets, just us and a ball. We played every chance we could. I was getting better at carrying the ball and receiving.

My routine that first fall was to go to school, come home and take care of the animals and then sneak off and play football. I was running around with several of the older guys. I started smoking more, cussing, and just acting like them. I found out later that they were into stealing at night. That was something I wouldn't do. I knew it wasn't right and if my dad found out, I was gonna get a beatin' for sure!

As the weather got colder and we waited for the bus, some of the other kids and I would go into the station. We would watch the people that owned the store play cards. They had a little café- coffee shop in there and you could buy a few groceries. I soon found out that their card games were for real. They were playing for money. They had a system where they played for match sticks, then would settle up with real money at the end of the game. Once in a while, the police would raid them. In those days, gambling was against the law. They would get a 'heads-up' call from someone and then they would put everything away and be playing euchre when the police arrived.

A Business Enterprise

One day, I went inside to warm up. I bought a nickel pack of chewing gum and on the way to school, I popped a piece in my mouth just before I got on the bus. Everyone around me wanted a piece. I only had 4 pieces left.

"Well, if you want a piece, you will have to buy it because there isn't enough to go around."

One kid offered me a nickel for one piece. Wow! The entrepreneur in me came out in full force. I started buying packs of gum and selling it on the school bus and at school. That one nickel started it all. It was a way for me to be able to buy lunch or at least part of a lunch. Most of the time before that, I had to sit in the gym during lunch because I didn't have money to buy it.

For a young growing boy not to be able to eat lunch with the rest of the class was torture. I had to go without a lot, but now, if I could find an empty pop bottle, I could sell it back to the store. I could use that money and buy two packs of gum, sell them at a nickel a stick and I had money for lunch. It was a pretty lucrative business most of the time.

We continued our football games whenever we could, but it was getting a lot colder outside. The ground was frozen and when you got tackled or fell on the grass it hurt. But, we kept on playing until the snow came. The weather turned bad and we were all stuck at home trying to survive the winter. That is the way winter is in the Midwest, survival! We spent our time trying to make sure the animals were ok and surviving.

Throughout the winter, we boys would see each other on

the bus, but the other guys were older than I was. Once we got to school, they were in another hall of the school and I didn't see them much. I could tell things were changing. The big kid from that first day on the bus had started turning them against me. He wanted to be the cool guy and he was telling lies or whatever he could to cause me problems. He pretended to be my friend. Even though we sometimes played basketball at home in the evenings or on the weekends, I could just tell he was doing things behind my back. He was trying to cause me problems.

Summer finally arrived. We were finally free of school. I'm a farm kid and I like to be outside, so school was rough for me. For the first time in my life, I would take care of the livestock in the morning be done in just a few minutes. I often found myself with nothing to do. It was a strange feeling and I got bored.

It wasn't long before I started running around with the older kids in town. Of course that big kid was there all the time. He tried acting like everything was just fine. I started noticing that other kids were starting arguments. I found out that the big kid was fueling the fire and starting those arguments. Before I knew it, I had to fight guys that I once thought were my friends. One after the other they came at me. I wasn't sure what was going on. They were all a couple of years older and bigger and much stronger than I was. I held my own for the first couple of fights because they were with the smallest of the older guys. I didn't win, but held my own. It was a rough time for me. I just didn't seem to fit in anywhere.

The Fish Fry

Every spring or early summer, the local volunteer fire department would have a fish fry to fund the fire station. I had never even heard of a fish fry before. People came in from all around the county. It was packed with people. They had tractor pulls and games. Kenny and I went downtown to check it out. We thought it was pretty neat. Later that evening, they had people singing and a band playing music.

Later in the evening, we went home for supper. By the time we finished, it was dark, so I headed over to see what else was going on. I took the short cut through the parking lot to see what was happening on the stage they had setup. As I got about halfway through the parked cars, someone grabbed me from behind and had my arms locked behind my back. That same kid from the bus and all the guys I had been hanging around with came out from the cars.

"We are going to kick the crap out of you."

The kid drew back to hit me. I used the guy behind me as leverage, flipped my legs up and I kicked him as hard as I could in the chest and again in his face. Then I felt a punch in my ribs. Someone had hit me from the side. I tried to kick, but there were five of them. They beat me in the stomach and the ribs until I couldn't breathe. Then, suddenly the guy who had me by the arms let go and I dropped to the ground. I was pretty beat up and was definitely hurting. The thing that hurt the most was my feelings. These were guys I had thought were my friends. I wasn't sure why they had done this to me.

As I made my way home, a fury came upon me and I was raging inside. They were all a lot bigger than me, yet, they were such cowards. It took all of them ganging up on a smaller kid (Me!) to beat him up. By the time I got back home, I was out for blood. I snuck into my mom and dad's bedroom and pulled out the drawer where Dad kept his pistol. I knew right where it was. I took it out, dropped the chamber open to make sure it was loaded, and slid it into my belt. I pulled my shirt down over it and headed out of the house. As I started across the front yard Dad yelled at me.

"Hey, where you think you're going?" Dad asked.

"Oh, I'm going back over to the fish fry to hear the music with the guys."

"What's the matter with you, you hurt or something? You don't look like your walking right."

"Oh," I said, "I fell down, but I'm ok."

"Come here, let me look at you."

When I got about ten feet away from him, I stopped.

"What's the matter with your face? Come over here into the light. Oh, so you fell, huh? It looks to me like you got beat up. Who did this to you?"

"Some older kids."

"How many older kids?"

"There were five of them."

He looked at me and saw the bulge in my belt. "What do you have there?"

"An equalizer."

Dad made me pull up my shirt and saw his pistol I was hiding. He took it away from me immediately.

"Give that to me. You can't do it that way. You have to catch them one at a time and hit them before they know you are even there. If you can't beat them with your fists, then you have to wait until you get older and closer to their size. You need to think this through, son."

He took the gun back in the house and put it away. As he

walked back toward the house, I was so mad I couldn't control myself. I walked over and found the axe that was leaning by the garage. I had just put a new handle in it. I picked it up and I broke the handle out of it. I took the broken handle and started back to the fish fry. Once again, Dad stopped me as I got to the edge of the yard.

"No, son. You are not going to do it that way."

Dad made me come back into the house. When we got inside, Mom saw me and could tell I was upset.

"What happened to him?" she asked Dad.

"We can talk about it later," Dad replied. "Raymond, go into the bathroom and clean yourself up."

I did as he said. When I got into the bathroom and looked in the mirror, you could definitely tell I had been into a brawl. I cleaned up my face as best I could. You can't clean bruises or swollen red places. I removed my shirt and found that I was pretty banged and bruised all up and down my ribs. By the time I got cleaned up and came out of the bathroom, Dad had told Mom what had happened.

"Let me see your ribs," she said.

I pulled up my shirt and revealed my bruises to her.

"Let's wrap you up tight, so it doesn't hurt as bad."

She took part of an old sheet and wrapped around my ribs tightly. She pinned it so that it wouldn't fall off. I was amazed at how much that helped. It still hurt badly, but it was better. Moms have a tendency to make everything better.

I walked into the living room and placed my hand on the doorknob. I started out the door.

"Where do you think you're going?" Dad asked.

"I have to go back over there Dad. I can't let them think that they can make me afraid of them."

"I understand," he said.

Mom was absolutely against it and said so.

"You want me to go with you?" Dad asked.

"No, I can't do that. I have to handle it myself or I will look like a coward."

"Well, you go, but don't try to fight them again. You are too banged up. Go get Kenny and take him with you. Be sure you stay out where you have plenty of light and where there are lots of adults around. Stay out in the open. Don't go where they can get you alone. Stay on the street."

I agreed. I grabbed Kenny and we headed out. As we walked over, I was nervous. I expected trouble at any time, but we arrived safe and sound. When we got back over to the fish fry, we did as Dad said. We stayed in the group of older people. I looked over and there came trouble and his friends. I say his friends, because they were no longer friends of mine.

"What are you doing here?" he asked. "I thought we

taught you not to come around here."

"Yeah, well, you and your friends don't run this little town. I go where I want and when I want."

I could see the shock on his face. He was taken aback. He wasn't expecting to see me back there.

His friends asked, "So, what? Did you tell the police?"

"You know I didn't tell the police, but that's a good idea."

They looked at Kenny and said with a smirk, "Is that your bodyguard?"

"No, he's my brother. But, at least he isn't a coward who has to fight five against one."

Just then, some older men who were standing nearby, came over and started talking to me. They were Dad's friends and happened to see what was going on. They asked if I would help them put up hay over the summer.

Kim chimed in, "We can help you"

But the guy said, "No, we just need these two boys to help, they are farm kids."

Since the farmers weren't giving them any time or attention, Kim and his friends left.

After that night, I knew I had to watch my back at all times. Every few days it seemed I would have to fight some kid that the kid had sent to confront me.

Granddad Intervenes

About three weeks later, I was walking to the store and my granddad pulled up in his pickup alongside me as I was walking.

"I hear that you don't have enough to do?"

"Huh!"

"Yeah, you're a farm kid and have always had to work hard. I heard you been getting into trouble because you don't have enough to do."

"I'm not in trouble."

"Well, I hear you've been fighting every kid in town and some of them two or three times. I think you need to come down and stay with me and Grandma and help me on the farm. You take care of the livestock for your room and board and anything I need done in the fields I will pay you for."

"We will have to ask Mom and Dad. What will they say?"

"I already talked to them and they think its ok."

So I moved to my granddad's farm.

My granddad had a nice place. He had built a new, large brick house and a tool shed to work on his equipment. Later, he built a new pole building for his cattle. The house was real nice. It was a large three bedroom ranch on a full basement. The basement had a second kitchen where my grandma did all of her cooking. It had a dining area and a large family room with a big brick fireplace. It also had a bedroom for me. I had a bedroom all my own. My grandparents slept upstairs.

My uncle lived with my grandparents. He had been paralyzed in a car accident years before. He had the bedroom upstairs, next to them. Grandma always kept the upstairs very tidy. My grandmother said that she had raised kids and now she wanted a place for company to come. She didn't want to worry about her house not being clean and orderly.

It was nice to come in the evening and have supper waiting on me. After supper, Grandpa and Grandma would go upstairs and watch TV in the big living room. My uncle had a TV in his bedroom and sometimes I would watch TV. Otherwise, I would watch it down in the basement. The basement was like my own apartment.

I helped my granddad farm and was around my uncles most the time. They became like older brothers to me at least the younger ones were. I would help them farm, cut wood or whatever needed done. It was great being able to grow up and learn from them. Two of my uncles were twins. They were very influential in my life; not always in a good way. But, I'll talk more about that later.

My granddad was a special guy. He had a wealth of wisdom that he shared with me. It was comforting to know that he could teach me something and if I messed up or didn't understand, I didn't have to worry about getting hit. He had a lot of experience with kids. He and Grandma had raised twelve kids of their own. He and Grandma had also taken in stray kids off and on through the years. I don't think I could count all of the kids that had stayed with my grandparents in just my thirteen years and now I was one of those strays.

My granddad and I became very close. He taught me about farming, about life, and he taught me how to become a decent human being instead of a rogue. Life was good. I did my work and had plenty to eat. My grandma was a great cook. I had more food than I could ever remember having. I never went hungry.

I had my own little apartment setting at night. I spent time with my uncle who was paralyzed. He had been injured in a car accident when he was twenty-one. I helped him and helped my grandmother to move him around. My other uncles, who were grown and out of the house, would come over and get me. They would take me places with them. I got to go to farm implement shops and restaurants. I had become a pretty good farmhand and tried to offer my services to them on their farms. It was a good time in my life. I still went to school and had to deal with the kids from the little town we lived in, but life was better than it had been.

Most of my time was spent at my grandparent's farm. I would still have to stay at Mom and Dad's some, because they said they missed me. When I would be at Mom and Dad's it seemed I always was able to find some kind of trouble to get into.

The Harley

We had moved the two cows that Kenny and I owned down to Grandpa's where they had a better pasture. Jeanie, our cow, was soon with calf again. While I was running around with my uncle one day, we had stopped at an old farmer's house my uncle knew. While they were talking, I saw an old Harley Davidson motorcycle in his barn.

""Hey, what's up with that motorcycle?" I asked him.

"It ran before, but it hasn't run for quite a while."

"Well, would you be interested in selling it?"

"Yes, I think I would."

"What would you take for it?"

"Oh, probably a couple of hundred dollars."

"I don't have a couple of hundred dollars right now."

"Well, I'm looking for a good milk cow, so I need the money to buy one."

My mind was whirling. It just so happened that I had two milk cows. When we went to Dad and Mom's the next time, I talked Kenny into selling me his half of the cow for the money I had saved from working. I traded the old farmer the cow for the motorcycle. I was more than excited to have my own motorcycle. I had one problem, however, my cousin had been killed in a motorcycle accident a year and a half earlier and my grandma wouldn't even hear of me having it, nor would she even allow one on the farm. So, with the farmer's help I finally got the motorcycle started and I rode it down to Dad's.

When I pulled up in the yard, I got it stopped just fine. When I put my leg down off the foot peg, so I could put the kickstand down, my leg wasn't long enough. I had all the weight of the bike on me and I had to let it down on its side. I quickly got off and picked it back up. It took everything I could muster just to get it up on its tires. I got the kick stand down and let it down on the stand. Sheeeew! I quickly looked around to see if anyone was around and had seen the incident happen. I didn't see anyone, then I looked up at the front door. There stood my dad looking out at me.

He came out on the front porch, spat a big glob of tobacco spit in the yard and said, "Boy, what are you doing with that motorcycle?"

I proudly proclaimed, "I bought it."

"How did you get it here?"

"I rode it."

"Well, you don't have a driver's license and no plates on it. Did you get a title for it?"

I quickly reached into my back jeans pocket and said, "Yep, see."

He came down off the porch and started walking around the motorcycle checking it out. I thought, '*Oh no he's going to make me take it back.*'

"How did you pay for it?"

"I bought Kenny out of his half of the cow and traded the cow for it."

He looked some more then he threw his leg over the side of it and sat down.

"This is too big for you, but it's just about the same size Harley I had as a young man."

My heart sank. I could see his countenance change. He wasn't interested in me taking the bike back, he was wanting it for himself.

"What did your grandma say about you getting a bike?" he asked.

"I didn't tell her, that is why I rode it down here, so that she wouldn't know."

"Well, it's your bike and you can leave it here. We will fix it up, but you won't be able to ride it for a while, not until you get bigger. It will need to be ridden once in a while, so I can take care of that for you."

He did ride it *for me* and it always made me nervous because he wouldn't get it out unless he had been drinking. I was always afraid he would get in an accident like my cousin had.

When my uncles heard that I had bought a motorcycle, they were all interested in seeing it. After they found out what a deal I had gotten on it, they were pretty impressed. I cleaned the old bike up and waxed the tank and fenders. I polished the chrome and it actually looked pretty sharp. The paint shone and so did the chrome.

One evening, three of my uncles came over and they wanted to see my motorcycle. So, they headed to Dad's place. Dad had already been drinking and when my uncles arrived, they drank a bunch more. I pulled the motorcycle out of the garage they were all over it!

"Wow! We would have done anything to get a bike like this when we were your age," they said. "Why don't you fire it up?"

I put it in neutral and kicked a few times. It fired up and

rumbled to life. A Harley has a very distinct rumble when it runs.

"Well, ride it around."

"No, he can't take it out on the road. He doesn't have a license. But, I can show you. Move over, Raymond," Dad said.

I protested because I was afraid for his safety, but he wasn't listening. As I moved over, he threw his leg over the seat. Away he went showing it off to my uncles. He made several trips up the road and back, then he pulled in, grabbed another beer and motioned to my uncles

"Watch this!"

He took off up the road again. We were all sitting on the porch waiting for him to come back. I had a sick feeling in my stomach. I knew he was up to something stupid. Down the road he came. He was standing up on the foot pegs running about 40 mph. He cautiously put one foot on the seat then he climbed up, standing on the seat of the motorcycle at 40 mph. He raised his beer up to his mouth and he kind of wobbled. Suddenly, he got into some pea gravel on the road across from us. He wobbled again and the bike slid out from under him. Down he went into the pea-gravel on his butt. Dust flew and the motorcycle slid in front of him. He must have slid twenty-five or thirty feet.

We all jumped and ran over to see how bad it was. When

he got up, the gravel had torn his clothes off, revealing his back side. He quickly grabbed at the remnants of his clothing to cover himself. He headed for the house. As he walked away, we could see that the clothes weren't all the gravel had torn up; he had a severe case of road rash all over his butt and back.

I quickly started looking at how badly the bike was torn up. My uncles were laughing so hard at the image of Dad grabbing what few stitches of clothes he had, as he had scurried into the house. I quietly and angrily pushed my motorcycle over to the garage. My uncles went into the house to check on Dad. Soon, they came back out to the garage. They started helping me clean the bike up. It had broken the clutch handle and bent the gear shift against the motor.

"Don't worry Raymond, we can fix that up."

They worked with it and got it rideable again. I did have to get a new clutch handle and a cable, but at least Dad wouldn't be riding it again anytime soon.

Motorcycle Racing

Once I was finally able to start riding the motorcycle, some of the other kids in town had gotten small motorcycles. We started racing around Dad's property. We would ride around and around. It was fun and very competitive. I enjoyed the competition. We moved from that to drag racing the bikes. We found a cliff back by the river and tried our hand at hill climbing. I learned for the first time that it wasn't as easy as the guys on TV made it look. It also hurt a lot more when you didn't make it up the hill and the bike flipped over backwards on top of you. Like I said, we were competitive, so we kept trying. We finally agreed that getting hurt just wasn't that much fun. We still enjoyed racing around Dad's place.

Every so often, I would sneak my bike out and ride down the back streets of town. It would fly when I took it out in the open. I could get it up to about 80 mph. One day, while Dad was at work, I slid the Harley out of the shed. Mom was busy in the front of the house. I quietly pushed it out of the yard and down the street. I fired it up and away I went. It felt good to have the wind blowing on me and feeling the power of that old motor as I gave it more gas. As I got to the end of the street, I was having a blast. Now remember, I still didn't have a driver's license. As I turned the corner, there sitting in a driveway that was all grown up was a sheriff's car. I looked at them and they definitely saw me. I knew I was in trouble.

No license, no license plates and I was probably running sixty in a thirty-mile-an-hour speed limit. I quickly turned another corner and cranked it back full throttle. I braked quickly and turned down a gravel alley. I could see the Sheriff's car speeding down the street. They were trying to cut me off. I changed gears and hit the throttle so fast that that old bike was moving like a racing bike. Hey, I had all that practice, we had been racing all summer long. I made a couple more quick turns through a neighbor's yard. I rode that Harley right into our shed and shut it down. I closed the door put the lock on it and ran into the house. I sat down in the living room, trying to act as though I was stretched out and about to fall asleep.

I saw two cops walk up on the front porch. They knocked on the front door and it wasn't a friendly knock. I could tell they were mad. Mom came from her bedroom and answered the door.

"Can I help you?"

"Ma'am do you have a young son here about 14 or so years old?"

"Why, yes I do."

"Where is he now?"

"He is sitting right there watching television."

She pointed at me.

The officers looked in and asked, "Does he have a motorcycle?"

"Yes, he does."

"Has he been riding it today?"

"No, he's been right here watching TV and helping me."

"Can we look at the motorcycle?"

"Why sure. It's out in the shed out back."

I followed and we all went out to the shed. They saw the big lock on the door of the shed and asked, "Can you open the lock?"

"Raymond, go get the key for them."

"Ok," I said. When I went into the house, I acted like I was looking for the key, but I was trying to gather my thoughts on what I would say. After a few seconds, I went back out and said it's not there. I think Dad has it because he didn't want me to get into the shed."

"Oh, yeah, he probably did take the key."

Dad had taken it. He didn't want me leaving the shed unlocked so that someone could steal his tools. What Dad didn't know was that I had a duplicate key made at the hardware a few days before.

"Ok, are there any more kids you know of who have motorcycles around town?"

"Oh, yes, they are all over town. All the boys have them."

With that, they looked at me and said, "Do you know who it might have been?"

"I was watching TV."

They gave me real hard look and said, "Stay off the road with that motorcycle till you get your license,"

"Oh, don't worry, I will."

As they left, Mom said, "They have a lot of nerve. That kind of makes me mad that they thought one of my boys would be doing stuff like that."

Mom went back to her work and I was able to breathe again.

Even with the close call I had with the law, I would still sneak the bike out once in a while. I enjoyed taking a ride out through the country. It was nice to be able to have a way to go visit my friends or just take a cruise out on the road. I would often think about riding it across country when I got older.

Summers Spent Talking to God

Every summer was the same, I spent most of my time working on the farm with my granddad. My uncles would have me help them whenever my granddad didn't need me. I enjoyed working with them; they would take me places when they went. As I said before, I would go with them to the farm equipment dealerships, garages, even a restaurant once in a while. They would give me cigarettes and sometimes share a beer with me. Things I shouldn't have been doing at that age.

For a fourteen-year-old boy, it was a good time. The days were long, I would help my grandma with my uncle, Jim, in the mornings and then go out and work in the fields. Grandpa bought a new Massy Ferguson tractor. It was great. It had a better seat on it and it was a different platform than the old Allis Chalmers tractors that I had been used to. I would sit on that Massey and plow, disk and cultivate the fields all summer.

It was good sitting out there on that tractor, working the fields. It gave me time to think about things to consider my future. It also gave me time to think about nature. Most importantly, I had good influences in my life. Granddad would read his Bible in the evenings after supper and share what he read with me. It gave me time to reflect on what he told me and communicate with God. I had always known that there was something more than just this day-to-day life for me. God had something great for me to do. I was sure of that.

Being around animals every day, seeing all the trees and nature there as I worked the fields, let me feel that there had to be something more than happen stance that created all of it. It was just too perfect to not have been planned. I had always believed in God, He had even spoken to me in that hay field years before. But, sitting out there on that tractor plowing or whatever I was doing, gave me time to really ponder it. After a while, I started communicating with Him on a regular basis. I would talk to Him while I was out there alone. I would tell Him all about my plans. It made me feel closer to God. It was a good time in my life. I worked hard, but I could see what an impact I was making as those crops started to grow and then when we harvested them I saw that it paid for my grandpa and grandma to live.

My First Car

When I was fifteen, my uncle Dan had a good looking Burgundy 1966 Ford Thunderbird. It was sharp! It had wrap around leather bucket seats and the lights on it were so cool. The turn signals would cascade to show the direction he was driving.

He stopped by one afternoon and said, "Do you want to drive."

"Sure, I would love to."

So, we took off with me behind the wheel. That car just floated down the road. I had driven lots of trucks and even driven a few cars before, but this thing was the fanciest, best looking car I had ever driven. My Uncle Dan was only ten years older than me and he was as close to me as an older brother. Uncle Dan had a twin brother, Dave. But, he lived further away and I didn't spend as much time with him.

Uncle Dan said, "You're going to have to start saving some money you know? In another year you are going to be wanting to buy a car of your own."

"Yeah, I know, but I don't make enough. I don't have that kind of money."

Little did I know that he was going to spring a surprise on me later that year! About six months later, Uncle Dan stopped by.

"Hey Raymond, a friend of mine has an old Plymouth for sale. He is selling it for about two-hundred dollars. I was thinking I might buy it. You think you might be interested in it?"

"Maybe, but I don't have that much money."

Back then two-hundred dollars was a lot of money, especially for a kid.

"I'm thinking maybe we can work out a trade."

"What kind of a trade?"

"How about we trade your motorcycle for the car? I've been wanting a motorcycle."

I thought it over (with him coaxing me quite a bit, I might add).

"The car would be a lot better in the rain," he said.

I had been caught in some downpours while riding over to my friend's house. The rain felt like needles hitting my skin. Also, wintertime is a no-go. I wouldn't be able to ride my Harley when there was ice or snow on the roads. I couldn't even haul my friends around on the bike.

"OK, it's a deal."

I agreed even though I didn't even have my license yet.

A couple of days later he brought the old car over to Grandpa's house. It was a 1963 Plymouth Fury 3. It was red and was a four door. I looked inside and noticed the seats were ripped up and the car was filthy. I was disappointed to say the least. Evidently, his friend hadn't taken very good care of it. The paint was dull and dirty. Honestly, this old car looked like crap. But, it was mine.

I jumped behind the wheel and checked it out. Grandpa and Grandma said I would have to keep the car at Dad's house until I got my license. I think they knew if it was there, that I would be tempted to take it for a spin once in a while.

We started it up. I looked all over the place for the gear shift. I couldn't find it. It wasn't on the column and it wasn't on the floor. Uncle Dan could tell what I was doing.

"What's the matter?" he asked with a smirk on his face.

That smirk let me know that he knew something that I didn't.

"Looking for the shifter?"

"Yeah, where is it?"

"There is a little lever on the far left side of the dash."

I looked and discovered that it was the parking lever. There were buttons that you had to push in. R for reverse, L for low, 2 for second, D for drive and N for neutral. I pulled the lever down and pushed the R button the car started to back up, I slowly turned the wheel hit the brake and pushed the D button it started going forward.

"Ahhhh, I got it!"

We went for a little drive with Uncle Dan following me down the road to Dad's house. Dad was outside when we pulled up. He walked over to the car and looked it over.

"Whoa, that thing looks like it has seen better days."

"Yeah, I know, but I will clean it up and get it looking better. At least it's mine."

The next couple of days I stayed at Mom and Dad's house. I washed that old car about five times and it looked better each time I washed it. The paint was still dull, but it was better.

I walked down to the service station and asked some old guys who were there, "How to get the gloss back on paint? I just bought an old car and I need to get it shining again."

"Well," they said, "Most people wax their cars. You need some good wax."

They pointed out a couple of brands on the service station shelves.

"These would probably work best," they said.

I bought one of the cans of wax. I took that stuff home and read the instructions. It was a thick, heavy paste wax. I started waxing the car. It seemed like it took forever to get it on the car. I mean, it took hours and hours of elbow grease to put it on and even more to get it wiped off. When I was done that old car sparkled. You could see your face shining in it.

Next, I started cleaning the inside. I started with the floors. They were absolutely filthy. There was mud and grease packed and pressed into the carpet. I got a stiff bristled brush and some dawn dishwashing liquid from Mom. I got to work. I scrubbed and scrubbed. It was soaking wet when I was done, but it looked better. I left the windows down and let it dry.

I had worked all afternoon. I went inside and I was completely worn out from cleaning the car. The next morning, I got up and hurried outside. That old car looked as good as it possibly could. I slowly opened the door and looked at the carpets. Hey, those carpets were actually red, just like the car. They still had a little stain on them, but at least they were presentable and you could tell what color they were.

I started cleaning the dash and the gauges. They cleaned up pretty well, so I started working on the seats. Mom came out to check out all the work I had done.

"You know, I have some red thread about that color. Let me get it for you and see if we can sew those seats up."

She came back a few minutes later with a needle and some red thread. She stayed outside helping me sew those seats as long as she could.

It made a big difference where she had sewn. They really looked great. The parts I had sewn were not as good, but still they looked a lot better.

I did all the work and I couldn't even drive it yet. My car had to sit there in the front yard of Dad's place. I would go out and start it once in a while. I would even pull it back and forth in the yard, but I knew I couldn't take it off the property. I saved my money and went ahead and bought the license plates for it. I still didn't have any insurance for it. I would sit in it with the windows down dreaming of the day that I could take her out for a drive around town. Every once in a while, one of my friends would come over and check it out. I was the talk of the freshman and sophomore classes. I had a car!

I took Drivers Education class at school. It was fun. It let me get out of school for a few hours at least a couple of times a week. At the end of the semester I earned my driver's permit. This allowed me to drive with a licensed driver over the age of twenty-one as long as they were in the car with me.

Dad would let me take him to town, but, I had to pay for the gas. He just rode along, then he would have me pull into the bar where he usually went to drink. I sat outside while he drank beer with his friends. Every so often, he would bring a different friend out and show them my car. Sometimes, he was in there for hours drinking and talking. I was glad I had driven because, when he did come out he wasn't in any shape to drive. Nor was he able to give me instruction. I took it easy because if I did anything wrong, he would cuss and get upset if I didn't do things his way.

At least I got to drive my car into town and back. Mom would let me drive her around once in a while and even Uncle Dan rode with me some. Most of the winter though; my car sat in the driveway at Dad's house.

DeMolay

When I was fourteen, I was asked if I would like to join DeMolay. DeMolay is a group for boys fourteen and older. I decided to join, until I found out that you were required to pay dues. I didn't have the money for the dues, but I mentioned it to my Uncle Don. He was one of my dad's brothers. He was just a few years younger than my dad.

"I think it would be good for you. Since you helped around my farm some and stayed with my family when I had to work out of town, I will pay the dues for you," Uncle Don said.

I joined DeMolay. It was a good experience. There were several of the boys from all around the community. Some went to my school and some went to different schools. We would play cards, hold meetings and talk about things young boys talk about.

My Uncle Don's wife had a brother who was just a couple of years older than me. He had his driver's license, so I started riding with him to the meetings. The meetings were once a month. We would go out after the meetings. We would ride around, race other people, peel out in his car, stuff young boys like to do.

The next year, the group announced that they were going to go to Ball State University in the summer for a week for a state-wide meeting. There was a fee to go along and it was going to cost what seemed like a lot to me. The fee was fifty dollars. I had always wanted to go to college and the opportunity to visit sounded great. I had heard about the parties and drinking and the girls. Oh, yeah the girls!

I decided I was going to go on this trip, so I took on whatever extra jobs I could to raise the money. I even stopped spending money on the Plymouth, so I could go to this state meeting. When the time finally came to pay the fee, I had just made the deadline. So, with an extra twenty-five dollars in my pocket, I was ready to go.

When travel day came, I was very excited. My dad was driving me over to meet the other guys and he said something that caught my attention.

"I will make sure the old Plymouth is taken care of," he said under his breath.

"Dad," I said, "don't drive my car. The oil pressure isn't coming up where it should be and Uncle Dan talked to a mechanic about it for me. He said it had the oil pump filter blocked and not to drive it until I replaced it."

"Oh, don't worry about that," he said.

I could tell he was just saying that. I was afraid he was going to drive my car and destroy it while I was gone. We got to the drop off and everyone was excited. We were punching each other in the arm, like guys do. We were ready to head out on an adventure. I was excited, too, and soon the Plymouth was the last thing on my mind.

When we got to the college campus, it was great. They had huge high-rise dorms, and they put us in a girl's dorm with instructions that all the girls were gone for the summer, except the top floor and they had a special locking system. We were informed that they wouldn't be bothering us and it was stressed that we wouldn't be able to bother them.

We got settled in and went out for supper. They had a big cafeteria with all kinds of food and man, did we chow down! When we got back to the dorm, some of the college girls were waiting for the elevator to go to the top floor. They flirted with us a little and we flirted back, a lot. Our group leaders came up soon and we all went back upstairs to our rooms.

The leaders had really nice rooms at the other end of the hall from us. They had spent enough time with us for one day, so they went to their rooms and were talking and watching a little TV. Once we were in our room, we began to get settled in when we heard a knocking coming from the heater vent.

Then we heard a girl's voice saying, "Hey, are you guys interested in coming up and partying?"

We all said, "Heck yeah!"

We heard several of the girls laughing.

"Well, too bad, the doors are locked," they said and laughed again. "Well, guess we will see you tomorrow."

More laughter.

"Wait a minute! Let's talk," we said.

They talked to us and kept leading us on, for a few more minutes, then suddenly they said, "We have to go."

There we were, a bunch of teenage boys our testosterone levels raging through the roof and these college girls knew just what buttons to push. Our minds were whirling about these girls. Someone suggested we go on a Panty Raid. I hadn't even heard of a Panty Raid, let alone know what it was. But, hey if it involved those girls, I was in.

We started talking and planning on how we could get up

to the top floor. The elevator was not going to work because you had to have a code to ride it. There were security guards to worry about. So, we decided to go check out the stairs. We climbed the two flights of stairs and at the top, the heavy metal door was locked tight. Everyone was feeling pretty defeated. I think some of the guys were actually relieved because they had actually wanted to chicken out.

Me on the other hand, no way I was backing down. Growing up on the farm, I had been able to open locks a few times when we had lost the keys.

"I think I can pick that lock," I said.

"Yeah! Right…No way are you going to pick that lock," some of the guys said as they started back down the stairs.

I ran back down to the room and got a big heavy-duty paper clip from some papers I had. I began fashioning a lock pick out of the clip. I worked just a little while, wiggled the door handle a little and the lock turned. I pushed the door open.

The other guys yelled down the stairs, "Hey, you guys come back, Stanton got the door open."

They came running back up the stairs. We all went barging onto the girl's floor. There were probably eight or nine of us. As we walked down the hall, we found the room that was directly above ours. The room where the girls had been talking to us from earlier. We opened the door and there were three girls sitting there with their mouths open.

"Hey, how did you guys get the door open?"

I showed them the paper clip and they laughed. We hit it off with them right away. They took us down the hall to where there were other girls. Before we knew we had girls all around us talking to us. They told us that there was an older woman who watched over all the girls on the floor.

"You have to be quiet," they said.

We went into one of the rooms and were just getting to know each other when we heard her coming down the hall. One of the girls peeked out the door. She watched her come down the hall and when she went into another room.

"Hurry, get back down the stairs," they said.

As I was leaving, the girl I had been talking to, gave me a kiss on the cheek. Whew! I felt that kiss all night long. We got down the stairs, but I decided not to lock the stairway door back, just in case!

The next few days were interesting, to say the least. We had meetings during the day and at night we were left to sleep. There really wasn't much sleeping going on. We flirted back and forth with the girls upstairs. One night, they told us about a pizza place that was just off campus. It happened they were going to be there later that night. We made plans to go up to our rooms early and then when things got quiet, we would sneak to the stairway and out of the building.

That night, we went sneaking around to avoid security and whoever else might be looking for us. We got out without getting caught and when we got to the Pizza place it was full of college age people. They were drinking beer and having a blast. We settled in and crowded around a table. Those girls weren't there, but lots of other college kids were.

Feeling brave, I went up to the bar and ordered a beer. Much to my surprise, they served me. I went back over to the table, beer in hand. The other guys started going up and before we knew it we were in the midst of the party. After a little while we realized it was getting late and so we made our way back to the campus and started the sneaking process back to the dorm. When morning came it came very early and we were all a little hung over.

The next day, we all decided to go swimming. The leaders had given us the afternoon off and they offered several activities we could do. The school had a huge indoor swimming facility, so we went over there. It was great. It had a large, deep diving pool with the biggest diving platform I had ever seen. We jumped into the competition pool and were cutting up, rough-housing and having a great time. The Lifeguard was a beautiful college girl. I was flirting with her, heck we all were, but I was getting the most attention. At least I thought so at the time. I was trying to get more attention by acting like I was drowning. I was clowning around, but then I got a cramp in my thigh. It wasn't that bad, just a small cramp, but of course I made the most of it. I was yelling and carrying on. The beautiful Lifeguard jumped in the water and helped me out of the pool. Then she rubbed the cramp out of my leg.

"There, are you feeling better?" she asked.

"Yeah, but aren't you going to give me mouth to mouth?"

She just laughed, but she did give me a quick kiss on the mouth.

"Get out of here," she said with a laugh.

I was *The Man*. It was hilarious because all of the guys there were splashing around and acting like they had a cramp; to no avail. She wasn't buying it.

The next day we headed home. We'd had a great time. Each one of us had a story or two to tell. We were all tired. We had been having so much fun, we hadn't had more than a few hours of sleep all week.

When we arrived at our pick-up spot, Dad was there waiting on me. On the way home, he was especially quiet. I noticed it, but I was tired and just tried to catch a quick nap. When we pulled into the drive, I immediately noticed that my Plymouth was sitting at slightly a different angle than it had been before I left it.

"Hey," I said, "my car has been moved."

"Yeah, well, I wanted to talk to you about that," Dad said.

"What do you mean you want to talk to me about that?"

I knew as soon as he said it like that the next words out of his mouth were not going to be good.

"I drove your car to work one day and it didn't make it."

"What?" (He worked up on the other side of Indianapolis it was over 60 miles one way to work).

"I drove it a couple of days actually and it did fine. Yesterday, on the way to work, the motor locked up on it. It's done. But, don't worry we can go to the junk yard and get you another motor."

I was tired. I was also fuming mad. I had asked him not to drive my car while I was gone. I had told him that it needed fixed, and now the motor was shot.

Dad Gets a Motor

True to his word, several weeks later, Dad came down to Grandpa's and told me he had found a motor for the Plymouth. In fact, he had found several but he said he had just needed some time to save the money to buy one. I was living back at Grandpa's house permanently. There was no more moving back and forth.

I was still really steamed about the motor situation. But, I went with him and we went to the junk yard to look at motors. Unfortunately, by the time we got there, the price had changed on the motor, or so Dad said. They wanted more money for that particular one, but they said they had another one. We looked at it and decided it would work, so we bought it.

It was old and rusty, but they assured us it was in working order when they took it out of the car. We loaded it up and took it to Dad's house. I worked for the next two days getting the old motor out of my car and then Dad helped me get the new motor back in. We finally got the motor in and ready to start. One of Dad's friends from work dropped by and he helped us get it started. It ran, but it was really rough sounding. We adjusted the timing and the carburetor.

We pulled the car out of the garage without the hood.

"Drive it down the road and check it out," Dad said.

So, down the road I went. The more I drove it, the better it ran. When I pulled back into the drive at Dad's house, it blew the radiator hose off and started missing out. Dad and his friend discussed the situation and decided that it had a valve problem.

Next, we took the valve heads off and Dad's friend agreed to take the heads into his work and get them ground down and mill the heads to give it a little more horsepower. Three or four weeks later, after all the work of replacing the motor, Dad's friend finally brought the heads back. I spent all the money I had been saving for a new head gasket set. We put the heads on and fired the car up. It ran and it was better than it had been before, but the old motor still ran rough. The Plymouth was never quite right after that. I was very disappointed.

I finally got my driver's license and I pulled that old Plymouth out and was gone whenever I had a couple of dollars for gasoline. The push-button, automatic transmission buttons would occasionally come off and leave me stranded. I would have to take the dash apart at the most inopportune times just to get the car into gear. I soon became an expert at fixing the shifter buttons.

I began racing a few guys around town who had some older cars. I won a few and I lost many. Most of the time, it was the Plymouth bringing up the rear. A friend from school had been driving his dad's new Dodge Super B to school once in a while. Man, that thing was nice! It was sleek; it was powerful; and it was fast! It was a beautiful blue and had a white vinyl top. I rode in it a few times and knew I wanted one.

I started saving my money. One day, I saw a Super B at a used car lot in town. My mom happened to be with me. It wasn't as nice as the one my friend drove around, but it was nice. It was copper-colored and had a black vinyl top. We stopped to take a look at it. I talked with the salesman and he said he wanted fifteen-hundred dollars for it.

"Are you kidding me? Heck, you can buy a new one for twenty-three-hundred dollars."

"Hey, Mom, let's take it out for a test drive?"

I noticed right away that it had a rattle in the motor. I stopped and checked the oil and it was thick and heavy. I knew immediately that it hadn't been changed like it should have been. The car had hydraulic lifters, so when the oil is not clean, that meant it wasn't pumping up the lifters properly. That's why it made the rattle and knocking noise. We drove back to the car lot.

"Well, what do you think?"

"It's definitely nice, but the motor has a bad knock in it. It needs work on it. It may even need to be replaced. So, fifteen-hundred dollars isn't even close to where it should be on price."

The salesman wasn't expecting a sixteen-year-old kid to know that much about cars. He probably figured I had just gotten my license and was just trying to get the price down.

"Ma'am, I don't think he really knows what he is talking about here. This car runs great."

He tried to convince my mom that I didn't know what I was talking about.

Mom just looked at him with a frown on her face and said, "Sir, my son has grown up on a farm. He has been working on motors since he was a little boy. If he says it has problems, it has problems."

"Oh, I see. Well, what are you thinking the price should be?"

"I would go six hundred dollars," I said.

"How about a thousand?"

"No," I answered.

We finally settled for eight-hundred dollars. It was a much better price, but it was still a lot more than I had. I had one-hundred and thirty dollars to my name.

"Well, let us talk about it," Mom said.

"We will get back with you," I said.

As we were driving off, Mom and I were talking about the car on the way home.

"You know, Mom, that is a lot more money than I have. So, buying that car is not going to happen."

"How much can you sell that car for if you fix it up.?"

"Probably fifteen-hundred dollars. It would be worth what he was asking if it was fixed."

"Hmmm. And how much will it cost you to fix that motor?"

"The problem is, they didn't change the oil regularly, so I would need to flush the engine out with diesel fuel and then put in new oil and a new filter. That's really about all it needs, so about fifteen bucks."

She looked at me and smiled and said, "Really?"

"I think so. It just needs those lifters to pump up."

Later that evening, I was still at Mom and Dad's house. Mom called me into the house to talk some more about that car. Dad had gone to bed.

"I think we need to go to the bank tomorrow."

"Ok," I said.

I wasn't sure what she meant at the time.

The next day, after Dad left for work, Mom said, "Let's go to the bank."

When we arrived, we went in and she specifically asked for one of Dad's friends. This friend at the bank had loaned Dad money before. Mom and I walked into his office. He made some small talk and asked how we were and asked about Dad.

"So, what brings you into see me today?"

Mom started telling him about the Super bee. He listened intently, and asked me questions about it. He looked up what the car was worth and said, "Are you sure that's all that's wrong with the motor?"

"I'm pretty sure," I said.

"Here, sign this paper."

He slid a paper across the table to me. I signed it and Mom signed it. He handed me eight-hundred dollars and said, "Go get that car. You can make payments of fifty-dollars a month."

I was shocked, but coming out of that bank I was walking pretty tall. Mom was the one who had cosigned for me. She was starting me out on the right foot, building my credit. We drove into town and stopped at the car lot.

The same sales guy was there. "Well, I didn't think I would be seeing you again. I need to find something a little less expensive, I guess."

"No, we will buy the Dodge over there."

"Like I said, it takes eight-hundred-dollars to buy that car. I can't sell it without payment in full."

I pulled the cash out and waved in front of his face.

"Well, step into my office."

I filled out the paperwork, got the keys and I drove that car off the lot. I stepped on the gas, shifted into second gear and lit the back tires up. Just a little! Mom was following me in my Plymouth.

When we got home, Mom said, "Ok, get that motor flushed and get the new oil in that car before your Dad gets home, so it sounds like a new one."

I opened the garage doors, pulled it in and went to work. Once I had made sure the motor was cleaned out and poured the new oil in it, I pulled it out of the garage and let the car run for a few minutes. It had started out with the chatter still in it. Mom was sitting on the porch watching and listening as the oil worked its way up into the motor; the lifters started quieting down until all you could here was a powerful, beautiful motor rumble. I gently revved the motor a few times.

"Mom, get in."

We drove down the road and it acted like a totally different car. I kicked it down a few times with Mom in the car. She laughed and tried to maintain her composure, but she was having a blast. It was a rocket, but I didn't put the pedal all the way down. I didn't want her to know how much power it really had. That car was awesome.

Before long, I was racing that thing all over town. I actually was able to make money racing against other guys in town now that I had a car that would blow their doors off.

One evening, while I was in town, this older guy who owned the shell station, had a 'Cuda that he had built for the drag strip. It wasn't street legal, but he had heard about my car and said he wanted to race me. I was game, so, we raced right down through the main drag of town. He did beat me, but only by a couple of car lengths. I felt like I held my own. I was pretty impressed with myself and my car. Most of the guys who owned fast cars around town were there when we raced. In fact, they had blocked the road so we could race. I think they were impressed, too.

A few days later, I stopped in at the garage. There were a couple of guys just down the road who were great mechanics. They were there when I stopped in. I found out these guys built race cars and had even worked on pit crews at the Indy 500.

"So," they asked, "you know the guy with the Cuda?"

"Yeah, I know him."

"Will that car of yours beat his?"

"I just raced him the other night and he beat me by a just couple of car lengths."

"Really?"

"Yep."

"He was in here bragging about his car. We don't like that

s.o.b."

I didn't want to get into the middle of their quarrel, so I didn't say much.

"Bring your car around here and let's see what that thing's got."

So, I went out, got in my car and pulled it into their garage. They lifted the hood and looked around. They had me rev the motor a few times.

"Hmm," they said, "we can make this thing beat that s.o.b."

"I don't have any money to spend for parts and labor."

"That's ok. We will take care of it. You just blow his doors off when we are finished."

So, I left my car with them. I hung around while they worked late into the night and then drove me to my grandpa's house. I rode the bus to school the next morning while they worked on my car. I had promised that I wouldn't tell anybody about what they were doing. They didn't want word to get out about what they were doing.

When I got home from school a couple of days later, they pulled into Grandpa's drive.

"Jump in, we have your car done," they said.

I jumped in and we headed to the garage.

"Jump in and fire it up."

Man, it sounded great. It was louder and stronger sounding. I could tell when the motor turned over that they had boosted the compression. It took a lot more battery to turn that motor over now. It actually took so much battery, that if it didn't start after turning it over three times, the battery wouldn't turn it over at all on the fourth try.

We headed into town to buy a bigger battery. They bought a huge tractor battery and strapped it into my car.

"Now, just a reminder," they said, "don't tell anyone. We want you to just drive up to him and set up a race."

They told me what day they wanted me to set the race up for so they could be there. I did as they asked and this time that 'Cuda didn't know what hit it. He was pretty cocky, thinking he would blow my doors off again. We started out pretty close, but I blew past him at the end of the quarter mile. I beat him by about three quarters of a car length.

I'm pretty positive the guys had lots of bets on the side. I don't know how much they made, but they were friends of mine for years after that. I guess I made them proud.

Once the word got out about my 'Bad' car, girls would ask me to ride in the Super bee. I never did figure out if it was the car or me that they wanted to be with. I went on lots of dates, but eventually, I started dating a girl a year behind me in school. She was with me most of the time after school was out.

Her dad was not real happy about the situation, to say the least.

Back then, word was out that I was trouble. I guess he could tell and he didn't want his daughter with me. He had plans for her to become something special. I know because he made sure to take me aside and inform me. So, her parents set limits on how often we could see each other. We could get together one time during the week and once on the weekend and she always had to be home by 10. That worked out fine because she had band practice after school and volleyball practice and I just made sure to be there as practice ended.

I now had a nice car; was racing to pick up some extra money; was still working on Grandpa's farm and helping my uncles on their farms. I also started working at a local grocery store. You could definitely say I kept pretty busy. That was fine with me, I liked being busy.

From a young age, I always had this idea that I would become rich someday. I wasn't afraid to work hard. I had always worked hard. Things were going well for me. I was making enough money to keep up with the things I wanted and needed to do.

The fall of my senior year, there was a notice at school that Cummins Diesel Engine Company was taking applications from High School seniors and would be hiring in the spring. At that time, Cummins was the best factory job around. They had great benefits and good pay. I decided I would go after school and put in an application. The application time was limited and if you didn't get to apply when specified, it was hard to tell when there would be another opportunity.

I worked it out with a friend of mine from school that he would pay for the gas and I would drive us down to fill out an application. I was talking to my uncle Jim. I told him about going to apply for a job at Cummins the next day.

"I'd rather you don't go put in an application for Cummins," he said.

"Why?" I asked.

"I just have a bad feeling about it and I don't want you to go."

Uncle Jim had been in a bad car accident when he was twenty-one and it had left him a quadriplegic. He had been in the hospital for over a year and then transferred to rehab for a long time. My grandparents had taken care of him at their home since then. My uncle Jim and I got along well. I really thought a lot of him. He was part of the reason I was staying at Grandpa's. I was there to help lift him up and move him when needed.

We watched football, basketball and played chess together. He was a really smart guy.

"Uncle Jim," I said, "this is my opportunity, I have to go."

"I'm telling you, I don't want you to go."

"It will be fine," I answered, and left it at that.

I was determined, so the next day after school Terry and I jumped in my car and headed to Columbus, Indiana to put in the application for Cummins. All the way down to Columbus I kind of felt guilty but I was so focused on getting that application in, I ignored the feeling. As we arrived in Columbus, a nice looking Olds 442 pulled up beside me. You could tell he had done a lot of work on his car. He nodded at us and revved his engine. I knew exactly what he wanted.

"You want to run 'em?"

"Sure," I answered.

When we pulled up to the first light in town, he pulled up on the right side of me. We lined up our cards and waited for the light to turn green. When that light turned green we took off. The Super bee was running great. I was ahead of him by a nose in first gear. I shifted to second and shot ahead a car length. He pulled back up on my rear quarter panel, trying to catch up. I hit third gear and we were screaming down the road.

Then it happened! A couple of older ladies were in front of us in a Volkswagen Bug. They slammed on their brakes because they were afraid of missing their turn. So, they screeched to a stop. An older gentleman in a Dodge Polara behind them hit them in the rear.

I'm coming up fast in the Super bee, hitting about eighty miles an hour and climbing quickly. I saw what was happening and let off the gas pedal. I tried to pull over to the right, but there was the 442 I had been racing beside me. I had hit the brakes and down shifted into second but it was too late.

We hit with a sickening and horrible crash. Everything went black. The next thing I knew, I heard Terry yelling at me.

"Ray, Ray, are you ok?"

I kind of came around and noticed there was smoke and steam and debris everywhere. I looked over at Terry and he had blood all over his face.

"Come on, man, we got to get out of here."

I wasn't quite sure what was going on, but went along.

We were still in the car and although I tried to open the door, it wouldn't open. Terry was pounding on the other door, but it wasn't budging either. I started climbing out the window. He couldn't get the window down on his side so he slid over and I helped him out the driver's side. Still disoriented, we walked over to the side of the road and sat down. We sat there, looking at the wreck. My Super bee was crushed in the front so badly that the front wheels didn't even touch the ground. The hood and motor had been pushed up against the windshield. As I looked at the other cars, I noticed that the Dodge Polara was driven up into the back of the Volkswagen Bug and was only touching the ground by the rear bumper.

A cop came up to me and asked for my driver's license.

"You boys alright?"

"Yeah."

He looked at us and said, "Looking at that car, it's a miracle you boys weren't killed. The ambulance will be here in a minute, you guys are going to the hospital."

When the ambulance arrived, we were all put in. The two older ladies were placed in first then Terry and me. The EMT's were checking the older gentleman out who had been in the Polara.

The two ladies started talking and the one said, "Are you ok?"

The other lady said, "Yes, I am fine."

"Oh, doesn't your neck hurt?" she asked.

She looked at her a little weird almost as if she was telling her that it should be hurting.

Again, she said, "No, I'm fine."

Again the first lady said, "Oh, I bet your neck hurts. In fact, I'm sure of it."

I was aware that whiplash claims had just become a popular claim a couple of years before. Some people had won big settlements for claiming whiplash. I knew what they were up to, so when the EMT's came back and started asking them about how they felt, they both suddenly had severe neck pain. All the way to the hospital the EMT's were putting neck braces on them.

When we got into the emergency room, they took them right back. The hospital wouldn't treat us until our parents came in and signed papers because we were both only seventeen. You had to be eighteen to sign for yourself.

Terry's parents came in and signed for his treatment. He had crushed the dash all the way to the windshield face first and had cut clear through his top lip. It ran diagonally from his nose to the bottom of his top lip. His dad came in and was really kind to me. He asked how I was and sat with me until my dad got there.

When Dad came in he signed the papers. They asked what was hurting me, I had bitten through my bottom lip and my jaw hurt like crazy, I could hardly open my mouth. I asked them to x-ray my jaw, but they wouldn't. They said it was just my lip and gave me some instructions to rinse it with salt water and to stay home for a couple of days until the bruising on my body was better.

Man, did I have bruises. I was bruised all over my body. When I got back to Grandpa's and Grandma's they were beside themselves. I had never seen Grandma so upset. She had been crying, I could tell. The worry was quite evident on her face. She grabbed me and started getting me comfortable. Grandpa just talked to me making sure I was alright. He had been really worried, too.

Then, my uncle Jim hollered for me to come into his bedroom. As I walked into his room, there he was laying in his bed, unable to get up. He read me the Riot Act. He chewed me up one side and down the other.

"I told you I didn't want you to go. I told you I had a bad feeling about it and you went anyway. Look at you all banged up. Don't you know you could have been hurt badly? You could have ended up like me, paralyzed and not able to take care of yourself. Or worse yet, you could have been killed or you could have killed someone else."

As I write this, his words and the tone of his voice still ring in my ears. He's been gone for twenty-three or twenty-four years now. I still miss him. It is interesting that I can still hear his voice some forty three years later. I never forgot what he said. I realized how selfish I had been. I wasn't thinking about Grandpa and Grandma, my parents and him. I was just going after a way to make more money. I know now that there are more important things in life than money.

After a few days, I went back to school and saw Terry for

the first time after the wreck. He had stitches in his lip and it was red and swollen but, he was doing pretty well. I still couldn't move my jaw much and had to eat things I could get through a straw. Everyone at school had heard about the wreck and they were all asking all sorts of questions.

During my second period class, I had just sat down at my desk and a girl that was not only cute, but a very sweet person, asked how I was. She wanted to know how the wreck happened. As I talked with her, she offered me a piece of chewing gum. I slid it into my mouth, man it tasted good. I had to chew carefully because of my jaw. We talked for just a few seconds when the teacher came back into the room. The bell rang shortly and I sat there very gingerly chewing that gum. Suddenly, I heard a loud POP.

The next thing I knew there were people standing over me. I was on the floor, the teacher was saying, "Ray, can you hear me?"

I looked up and there were several people looking down at me. My jaw hurt like crazy. I was dizzy and felt like I had been kicked in the face by a mule. But, I could open my mouth now. It hurt but, somehow it felt a lot better. It seems that while I was chewing that gum, I had moved my mouth just right and my jaw had snapped back into place. That was the big POP sound; everyone had heard it. The school insisted that

I go to the hospital and get checked out again, since I had passed out when it snapped back into place. I had mentioned my jaw to the hospital when I was taken there after the wreck but no one would listen to me.

At the hospital, they finally took an x-ray. I waited while they checked out the results.

The Dr. came in and said, "How did you break your jaw."

"You mean it was broken?"

"Yes, in two places. But it is set back where it is supposed to be now and it looks like it is going to heal alright. You just need to be careful not to chew meat or gum or anything. If you can do that, I don't think we will have to wire it together."

I was mad that they hadn't checked it out right after the wreck, but then on the way back home I thought it was definitely for the best. If they had found it then, they would have done surgery and wired my mouth shut. That would have been bad, because I like to eat and I definitely liked talking to the girls at school (shoot I liked talking to girls anywhere). Having my jaw wired shut might hurt my stomach as well as my 'game'.

The next week, Terry came over to Grandpa's and picked me up since I no longer had a car. He had a nice older Chrysler, but it was yellow and had a black vinyl top. It was a big car, but it ran well. It rode like a big luxury car. In fact, it just kind of floated. We went over to Franklin to see some friends of his and on the way back we were driving on highway 44. It was a straight stretch of road, there was no traffic and so he opened it up.

We got up to 80, 90 and then one-hundred and up to a hundred and ten. I had a bad feeling.

"Hey, you need to slow down. There is a road up here just over the hill they can't see us coming," I said.

He didn't listen. He kept his foot in it and sure enough we came over the hill, a woman with little kids in the car eased out in front of us. There were two cars coming the other way. Terry swerved to miss the woman's car, just clipping her bumper on my side of the car. The impact forced us sideways, just a little. We hit both of the other cars coming at us, glancing blows. We went down into a field and started rolling over and over. Fence, fencepost, dirt all over, we ended up right side up but the car was destroyed. The other people came out of their cars to check on us. It was a mess. We had just survived two huge wrecks in less than two weeks. We were already bruised, battered and sore; now we were even more so. We were black and blue all over.

The deputy sheriff arrived and he took us to my dad's house. I was really mad at Terry. I had tried to get him to take it easy. I told him I had a bad feeling about it. I realized just how lucky we were. Then, I thought, no not luck. Luck is a chance thing. I knew that God had kept his hand on us and that it had to be Him and Him alone who had kept us alive.

At that time, I was just coming to the realization that God was looking and was watching over me. It had to be God. All of these things that I had that happened and I was still in one piece.

The Super Bee was totaled, so now I didn't have a car to drive. I had to ride the bus to school and I had to depend on others to take me anywhere I needed to go. By this time, my uncle Jim had a van. We drove him around in it, but he wouldn't let me drive it. He was still mad at me for not listening to him and he was trying to teach me a lesson. I understood that he cared about me and was hurt because I hadn't listened to him. However, it still left me without a vehicle.

No vehicle meant I could only date, at the most, once or twice a week. That was only when my girlfriend's dad said it was ok for her to come see me. She would come over and pick me up. We would drive out of eyesight and then she would get out and I would change places with her and I would drive her car wherever we were going.

A short time later, my brother Kenny bought two old cars from a guy down the road. Dad worked with this old guy and he had a white 1960 Chevy that looked ok, but had a bad motor. He also had 1959 Chevy that had a good motor and looked terrible. Kenny had planned on switching the motor over into the 1960. The guy was having some money issues and wanted to sell the cars for some quick cash. Kenny bought them both. He was only fifteen and couldn't drive yet, so I told him I would help him change out the motor and get it running if he would let me drive it. He said yes, so that's what we did.

We went to work right away and hauled those cars down to Dad's house. We pulled the motors, put the good one in the old 1960 and got it up and running. After all the work I put into the car, Kenny finally informed me that the only way I could drive it was if he went with me.

That meant any time the wheels rolled, I had to take him with me. That meant drive him to school and wherever else I went. I didn't mind, for the most part, but it also meant he had to go along on my dates, if I used his car. That, I did mind! It was not a good situation. I made it work, though, and I drove his old car around until he got his license, which was about 4 months later.

I graduated early, at about eight weeks before school let out. One day, Dad and Mom came down to Grandpa's and picked me up.

"We've been talking about it and with the money you got

from insurance out of the Super Bee, we realize that it's not enough to pay for a nice car. But, it would make a nice down payment on a newer car. Your mom has been talking to a lady at church. Her son owns the biggest car dealership in the area," Dad said.

"You ought to go in and talk to him to see what he has," said Mom.

It sounded good to me, so we went in and talked to the guy. He ended up selling me a brand new 1973 Cutlass Supreme Brougham. It wasn't even on the lot yet. I got to special order it. It took about six weeks to come in, but it was worth the wait. It was sharp.

I drove it to school the next day and everyone was standing around looking it over. Actually, when I noticed, it seemed that several of my friends at school got new cars for graduation. The main difference was, I had to pay for mine, myself.

I Will Graduate!

Finally, graduation day was approaching. It was just a week away. It had been a long, hard year for me. The principal at this school made an extra effort to make my life hard. He was a short, stocky guy, who had it in for me from the beginning of the year. First, he would not give me a school driving permit. He said I could drive only on the days I had to work after school. Well, I worked every day, so I drove every day.

He came up to me in the hall the second week of my senior year and started yelling at me saying I told you, you couldn't drive and frogging me in the chest. Frogging is when you take your fist and sticking the knuckle out on the middle finger just a little further than the other fingers, so as to make it more painful when you hit someone. He hit me once right on the sternum and then yelled and hit me again. I told him that in no uncertain terms not to ever hit me again. It really hurt and I could feel a rage welling up in me. He hit me a third time and when he did, something snapped. I hit him under the chin with a right upper cut with all my strength behind it. It knocked him off his feet and he hit the floor on his back. He slid about three feet.

He shook his head, trying to regain his senses and said,

"Don't hit me again. Don't hit me again or I'll make it very rough on you."

Several people had seen the incident happen.

My brother Kenny kept saying, "Oh, no, Raymond you're in for it now."

I left the principal laying in the floor trying to get up and went to my first class.

After that, I could see the hate in his eyes when he looked at me. It had all been his fault and everyone in school agreed with me. There was no reason for him to yell at me, none-the-less hit me. The news traveled through the school. By the time I got to my second class that day, everyone was asking me about it.

Every school day of my senior year, I would get to my first period class and after role was taken and the announcements were done, they would speak over the intercom, "Ray Stanton report to the principal's office."

I would go in and he always made sure he had two or three other male teachers in his office with him. He clearly didn't want to be alone with me. When I would get in the office, he would berate me for ten or fifteen minutes.

"Why don't you just quit, Stanton? I'm going to see to it you don't graduate, so you need to just quit."

Every school day, he put me through this same treatment.

Everyone knew what he was doing, even the teachers. One day, the guidance counselor came to get me in the middle of the day, to take me to the office.

When he came into the room, my teacher, Mrs. Tucker asked, "Is there a problem?"

"We are going to kick Stanton out for causing problems in the hall on the other side of school just before class began."

Mrs. Tucker took up for me immediately. "He couldn't have been causing problems because he was talking to me before class started, right here."

She liked me and she followed me down to the office and lit into the principal, telling him that he was making stuff up and she had been with me. It was a constant battle.

After Mrs. Tucker stuck up for me, the principal came up with a new strategy. It seems there was a rule that if you were called to the office, they could deduct a small percentage from your grade. So, once I figured that out, it meant that I had to make straight A's in order to pass my classes. He was trying to make it nearly impossible for me to graduate.

I had friends coming up to me and offering to help. The girl I was dating was a straight A student. She helped me most of the time. I had several others that volunteered just because they didn't like the way I was being treated. It worked! I was squeaking by and had a week to go when the guidance counselor came to me again. He asked me to step out into the hall.

"Ray they want you in the office. They are planning on kicking you out of school. If they do you won't be able to graduate," he said.

I was mad and started down the hall to the office, I had had enough this time, I was ready to beat the principal within an inch of his life.

The guidance counselor grabbed my arm and said, "Don't go, I think you need to go home and get your Dad to handle this."

I figured he was trying to help me so, I went out the other door, got in my car and drove home. Luckily, Dad was at home. I told him what was going on, I could see a fire come up in his face. I had been taking vocational classes at a different school. He said, "You go on to vocational school, I will take care of this."

I headed out the door got in my car and went to the next school that I attended. Looking in my rear view mirror, I could see Dad speeding up behind me and then turning toward the high school. All afternoon I waited for them to call my name and tell me to go home.

When I got home that evening, Mom looked at me like something big had happened, but when I asked, "What's going on?" she said, "Don't say anything."

The next morning Dad said, "Raymond, you go on to school. If anyone causes you a problem, you come get me."

"Ok, Dad," I responded.

I headed on to school. As soon as Kenny and I walked in, there were a bunch of guys who came right up to me.

"Wow Stanton, your dad came storming in here. The principal, the coaches and everybody went out the other door running. They all got in their cars and left. Your dad grabbed a male teacher, picked him up off the ground and pinned him to the wall. He yelled at him, 'Where is that principal?'"

I'm not sure exactly what happened, but I know that was the end of the problems I had with the principal.

I continued attending school until the last day. I went to graduation and when I got my diploma I checked it to make sure it was signed. It was, but the ink was still wet and it still has a smear on it to this day where, I put my thumb on it to check. I would say I made it, but it was close!

Married Life

The next summer, after graduation, just breezed by. I was working full-time and still helping Grandpa and my uncles. My girlfriend and I were still dating. The entire summer was kind of a blur. I had turned eighteen and so now I was an adult, according to the law. That wasn't too important except my girlfriend was still in school. Once classes started back up, she was in her senior year. And she was only seventeen.

In October, she told me she was pregnant. I was definitely not ready for that, but it was too late now. We hadn't been careful and it had happened. We talked and talked about it and decided we had to tell our parents. Mine, I wasn't too concerned about, but hers was a different matter. Legally, she was underage and I was an adult. They could send me to jail if they wanted and I was pretty sure her dad would do just that. So, we went over to her house together and told them. Her parents were devastated and her dad literally blew a gasket.

"Well," he said, "You made your blister and now you're going to have to sit on it. You're going to have to get married pretty quickly or everyone will know what happened."

So, that was my option marriage or jail and I knew it.

We opted for marriage. We planned the wedding, made

the arrangements and set the date. My friends even threw a bachelor party for me. It was just a few of us guys and my brother Kenny. We managed to get very drunk, probably the drunkest I had ever been. I was still drunk when we all arrived at the church and I got married.

We bought a new mobile home to live in. It was nice, but still just a mobile home. It was a cheap place to live and we made the best of it. Her parents even came over with some dishes and several other things to help us get started and set up housekeeping. We were actually pretty happy.

A few days after the wedding, she got sick and started having problems with her pregnancy. I called her mom and told her what was going on, she said, "Take her to the hospital, we will meet you there."

I got her to the hospital as quickly as I could. She was immediately taken back and they left me waiting in the waiting room for her parents. I needed to tell them what was going on.

After about fifteen minutes, a doctor came out and said there is a problem with the pregnancy and we have to take her to surgery now. We sat there waiting. It seemed like forever. Every few minutes, her dad would say, "This is all your fault. I should have never allowed her to be around you. You should have taken my offer… you should have taken my offer."

To clarify, shortly after I had bought the new Cutlass, he had pulled me aside and offered to pay it off for me, if I would get out of his daughter's life. I didn't take it.

The doctor came back out shortly and told us she lost the baby. When she was released from the hospital, we went back home. Her mother came over and stayed with her for a few days while I was working nights driving a forklift at a local factory.

Working the third shift, and being confined inside a factory all the time just wasn't for me. In the spring, my uncle Dan got me a job working for the construction company where he worked. At least now I was outside running equipment. I was doing dirt work, building roads and parking lots. It was good money and I enjoyed it.

After some time, they put me on a different crew. We were laying asphalt, paving those same streets and parking lots. The guys I was working with on this crew were definitely not the same type of smart capable guys I had been working with before. I soon found these guys didn't have much of an education and were scroungers.

This job was definitely not much fun. I had to work the back of the paver and I had to help shovel asphalt all day long. I hated it, but it was still good money. By this time, I was pretty down and out. I started drinking more and more. At only eighteen, I was going into the bars after work for a beer with the guys. Then, I would stop on the way home at a liquor store to pick up a six pack. I would drink three or four on the way home. When I got home I would eat supper and drink the rest of the beer.

My marriage was going ok at that point. She had just graduated from high school and landed a job at the local farm Bureau grain elevator store. I was still working construction.

Suddenly, my pay checks started bouncing at one point, so the bank called me. They had five of my paychecks that had been returned when they tried to clear them through the company I worked for. I called the office about it, they said they were having some problems, but would make it right.

We wised up and when we would get paid, we would send a couple of guys to the bank and to cash everyone's checks. This way the company's own bank wouldn't cash the checks, but we cashed our checks. Soon, even that was over. The company went broke.

It was winter and there wasn't much outside work in Indiana in the winter, so we were officially laid off. That was the good thing because I started drawing unemployment. It was ok through the winter because I drove a truck for my Uncle and picked up a little extra money when I could.

When spring came, there were no construction jobs

around. Construction work was really slow at that time. I was nineteen years old, married and I needed a job. My unemployment was quickly running out and I was desperate. I was looking for anything. I was unable to find a job even though I had put in applications all over. A friend of mine, Mike, said he had read an ad in the paper for insurance agents so we both went up to see what it was all about.

Selling Insurance

Mike and his twin brother, John, had been friends of mine since the summer before I was married. We drank together and always were good friends. John had even been the best man at my wedding. Mike and I went to Southport and talked to the guy about the insurance job. We found out there was no salary. It was a straight commission pay. So, if you didn't sell anything, you didn't make any money. It was also door to door sales of life insurance. Mike wasn't interested, but he wasn't married and he still lived with his mom. I really had no choice. I had a wife who was worried and my unemployment had run out. I took the chance.

The guy told me, "I will give you one week. Take this book and study it over the weekend. If you bring me five sales by Friday of next week great. If not, you can just turn the product catalog in and go back home."

He had told me to drive to Versailles, Indiana on Monday. I need to be at the Moonlight Motel by nine o'clock a.m. The supervisor would tell me what to do. On Monday morning I drove the two hours to Versailles and found the Moonlight Motel. I asked for the supervisor. A young, short, heavy-set guy came out along with two other gentlemen.

I introduced myself and talked with them for little while. They welcomed me to the team and then one of them turned to the others and laughed.

"The new guy has to room with Grif."

Then, they all laughed and said, "Yeah, the new guy rooms with Grif."

"Who is Grif?" I asked.

They just laughed and said, "Oh, you will see."

This elicited more laughter. A few minutes later, Grif came driving up. I was introduced to him and he seemed ok. Just your average middle-aged guy. He was about forty years old and he had the look of a high school coach or something. I didn't care, but it had me worried that maybe he was homosexual or something. I didn't know what was so funny.

The supervisor explained the procedure to me. He said we traveled to different towns. We started by first knocking on doors and asking them to buy insurance. He went over some of the types of insurance policies we offered with me. He gave each of the other guys an area to work in. He gave me the town of Dillsboro, Indiana.

Dillsboro is a small crossroads farm town with a few houses in it. When I arrived there, I had no idea what I was doing. I drove up to the first house, got out and knocked on the door. There was no answer. Then, I went to the next house and I knocked on the door. A little old lady answered the door. I was nervous, so with a little quiver in my voice I told her what I was doing.

"Why, son, you don't look old enough to be an insurance agent."

"Well," I said, "this is my first day."

She grinned and invited me in.

"Now, you tell me what policies you have to offer"

I opened the book and started showing her the pictures and the policies that were available. When I got to the cancer policies, she said, "Now, I would be interested in something like that. How much is it."

I explained the cost to her. I told her it was $42.50 a year.

"I will take that one," she replied.

I wrote up the application and she wrote me a check. I was ecstatic. I was about to hurry out the door when she said, "You know, I have a bunch of friends coming over in a few minutes, if you can stay, I bet they would probably be interested in that cancer policy."

"Oh, of course," I said. My ears perking up.

"If you would stay till they get here, you can tell them all about it."

"Sure, I can do that."

In just a few minutes, she had a whole house full of her friends over for a quilting party. She introduced me and had me start explaining the policy I had sold her. She actually did most of the talking. They brought out milk and cookies and I sat there with a house full of little old ladies. I ate and I took down their information one at a time. By the time I left I had sold seven cancer policies.

I was breathing a lot easier. It was around four o'clock when I was done. I was accustomed to working from six a.m. until about four or five in the evening. So, naturally, I thought it was time to head back to Versailles. I was one happy guy. I had made over two hundred and fifty dollars at one house and I was feeling good.

When I arrived back to the motel, there was no one there. Since I didn't have a key, I went downtown and found a little bar called the Palm Garden. It was just a little hole-in-the-wall place. I recognized the Supervisor's car outside, so I went in and sure enough there was the boss and Grif sitting at a table having a beer. I walked up and sat down.

"What are you doing back already?" the supervisor asked.

"Well, it's after five o'clock and that's when I usually get off work."

"Well, that's not the way this gig works. We don't quit until we sell something. So, unless you have sold something you need to get back out there and work."

Just as he finished speaking, the waitress came up and asked me what I wanted. I ordered a beer. She carded me and I handed her a fake I.D. that an older friend had given me. It was his old draft card. She said "Ok" and left.

I didn't like the way the supervisor had spoken to me, but I kept quiet.

"So, you're going to drink a beer and you haven't written any business."

"No, you just said if I hadn't sold anything I needed to get back out there."

Grif laughed and said, "What did you sell?"

"Well, I did sell a little bit."

The boss was all ears after I said that.

"What did you sell?"

"I sold seven cancer policies today. Oh, and the ladies said if I can come back tomorrow they will have some more of their friends talk to me."

"What! Seven policies?"

The boss about fell over in his chair.

At this point, I had earned their respect. They both started talking to me more as an equal. We sat there and drank beer well up into the night.

When we finally went back to the motel, Grif said, "Come on Ray. They said you're rooming with me. Let's get some sleep."

I still wasn't sure about this guy. After all the laughter I had experienced earlier, all kinds of things were going through my mind. We walked into the motel and he took the bed he wanted. I stripped down to my shorts and climbed into the other bed. I was exhausted. We talked for a few minutes, then Grif shut out the light.

I wasn't going to sleep at all that night. A few minutes later I heard the worse noise I think I had ever heard a human being make when they sleep. Grif was snoring so loud, I swear the windows rattled. I am not kidding, he could wake the dead with that noise. It was bad! I was pretty sure that was what the guys were talking about. I got a bum deal because I was the new guy.

I didn't sleep much at all. It was my first night away from home since being married and I had never been in a motel before. So, while Grif snored, I pondered all the things that had happened the day before.

The next morning I got up, showered and shaved, dressed and went outside. No one was up yet. I was used to being up early. Obviously, these guys liked to sleep in. Finally, after a few minutes they started rousing and came outside.

Oh, they thought it was funny.

"Wow, did you sleep out here last night."

"No, I slept in the room. I'm just an early riser."

They all started laughing, "Yeah, right. You're trying to tell us that Grif's snoring didn't bother you?"

"Well, it was pretty loud, but I made it through all right."

At breakfast we were all cutting up and they were all joking with me. I could tell they were starting to accept me.

Every day was the same, get up, go out to whatever area they sent me to and knock on doors until you sold something. I quickly learned you had to be pretty brave to just walk up to a stranger's house and start a conversation. It was even harder to get them to listen to you. It was harder, yet, to get them to buy something.

In the evenings, we would meet at the bar and drink a few beers. Then, we would head back to the room. I had never lived like that before. It was a new experience for me.

I didn't have much money, so I wasn't eating very much. I was always a big eater, so I felt half starved. By Friday evening, we all headed back to the office in Indianapolis and turned in our business information for the week. Everyone else was done and had left. It was my turn. I walked in and turned in my business report.

The manager said, "Hey, you didn't do too badly for your first week. He wrote me a check and told me I could cash it at the bank across the street. I had made about what I was making working my butt off in construction and this was a lot easier for me.

That next week I had a little more money to spend for expenses and so I was eating a little better. I worked a lot harder than the week before, but I was making fewer sales. About midway through the week, I felt like part of the team and the other guys were accepting me.

Pickled Eggs, Burgers and Beer

One night, we were at the bar drinking. Grif and I were talking and relaxing. I was hungry, so I ordered a cheeseburger. I was still hungry, so I ate another one. I ended up eating four or five cheeseburgers and was still hungry. I didn't want to spend all my money on food, so I stopped

We had been drinking for several hours and I was still hungry. I asked the bartender what he had to eat that was cheap.

"We have pickled eggs. They are two for twenty five cents."

"Ok, give me a couple of those. I will try them."

I must have eaten ten of those pickled eggs that night. They weren't bad.

We headed back to the motel and I crawled into bed and fell asleep. Around seven-thirty the next morning I felt these awful gas pains. I rolled over and pulled the cover off of me and let one rip. Grif was snoring. It was silent, but deadly. Oh, my, gosh! It smelled so bad that I was glad I hadn't kept it under the covers.

The smell was so horrendous it made my eyes water. I quickly pulled the cover up over my nose just so I could breath.

Grif was snoring loudly, as usual. Suddenly, the smell reached his nose. He stopped snoring mid-snore and coughed. He tried to clear his throat. He started making some really weird noises. He grabbed his throat with both hands.

"OOOHHH ! What is that?"

The expression on his face changed suddenly. He scrunched his face up

"Ooohhh! Ooohhh! Something's wrong….Oh! No, something's wrong!"

He started waking up and he began gagging.

"Ray, get up! Ray, Get up! Something's wrong. We gotta get out of here."

I was trying my best to act like I was asleep, but I know that I must have been shaking the whole bed trying to keep myself from laughing out loud.

"Huh? Huh? What's wrong?"

"Come on, we got to get out of here."

Just as I climbed out of bed, I let another one ease out. It was just as rank as the first one…maybe more! I quickly slid on some pants and went outside with Grif. Oh, my, what a stench. It was horrible in that room. Once we were outside, Grif knocked on the room next door and had the other guys get up.

"Guys, get up, hurry! Something's wrong. Our room has

the worst smell I have ever smelled in my life. Something is wrong, terribly wrong!"

The boss and the other two guys roused from sleep. "Oh, bull, Grif. What are you waking us up for?"

"Seriously, guys. Something's not right."

Grif convinced them to go in and check it out. They opened the door and went into the room. They practically ran back out. They were flailing their arms and covering their noses. They were coughing and gagging.

"I'm going to get the manager. We can't have that," the boss said.

Before I could stop him he went storming off to the office. While he was talking to the manager, we went into their room to warm up. They had a wall-type radiator heater.

The boss and the motel manager went into our room to check it out. I could hear the manager saying, "It must be the sewer system."

There I was standing by the heater in the next room when I felt another gas pain. Oh, it hurt so badly, I had to let it out. It just silently slid out right there in front of the heater. I swear it was kind of like a green fog of the nastiest smell you ever smelled. It just started covering their room. I quickly went outside and sat down in a chair. One of the other guys walked back into their room and came out gagging. He had tears running down his face.

"Oh no, now it's in our room. Oh, man don't go in there. I almost didn't make it out alive."

He told the motel manager and the boss.

"Whatever it is, it's spreading and it's bad. I just about didn't get out of the next room. I couldn't catch my breath," he said.

I was doing the best I could, not to fall apart laughing. One of the guys looked at me and said, "What are you shaking about?"

"It's cold out here and I don't have a shirt on."

I started back into our room to get my shirt and shoes.

"Ray don't go in there. It's dangerous. That stuff could kill you," said Grif.

"It's ok, I'll hold my breath."

By this time, I had to let another one. So, I held my breath, ran in, and grabbed a shirt and my shoes. While I was in there, I let another one rip and ran back out.

We all left the manager to worry about the problem. I didn't say a word! We headed to breakfast. As we were leaving, the manager had gone into the other guy's room and I heard him say, "I think it's coming from the heater."

We all rode to the restaurant together. No way, I could let one rip with us all in the car or they would be on to me. I held the gas as long as I could, then made an excuse that I had to get to work. Once I was away from them, I let another one go.

I never did tell them what really happened, but have told this story to my family many times over the years. Beer, cheeseburgers with onions and pickled eggs are a deadly mixture that should never be repeated. And I never have!

Grif and I ended up being really good friends. We worked quite a bit together and we would ride around traveling from one town to another selling insurance door-to-door. I was drinking more and more. We would start drinking early in the afternoon and would drink way into the night.

Grif had been a high school football coach and had played football in college. He was an interesting character and he always had a story to tell. He had always been an adventurous type of guy and so was I. So, even though he was over twenty years older than I was, we just hit it off. We would drink beer and sell insurance. Grif taught me all I knew about sales and he was a great salesman.

I would work out of town, all over Indiana and come home when I could. I would leave home Monday morning and drive back home on Wednesday evening. Then back to work on Thursday morning and head back home late Friday night. We would always stop in Indianapolis to turn in our business reports and get paid on Friday evening. Of course, several of us would find a place to drink a few beers before we headed home.

On the weekends I would be at home so I would spend some time with my wife and then I would head over to Mike and John's house. We would drink more beer. They even talked me into smoking some pot.

I never really liked the pot, but I did it to be social. We drank all weekend, and then on Monday morning I would drive to wherever we were working in the state and the process would start all over again.

In 1975, my wife got pregnant again and we had a little girl in October of that year. She was the apple of my eye. I had never before felt the way that little baby made me feel. I was a proud dad. She was such a happy little kid and so smart. I would take her with me wherever I went when I was home. It was fun watching her grow up. My mom watched her while my wife worked and every weekend was my time to spend with her.

I was doing pretty well financially and I bought a new car. It was a 1976 Cutlass Brougham. It was a beautiful car. Later that year, I bought a ford pickup truck. I got tired of living in a Mobile home park. It was a nice place, for what it was.

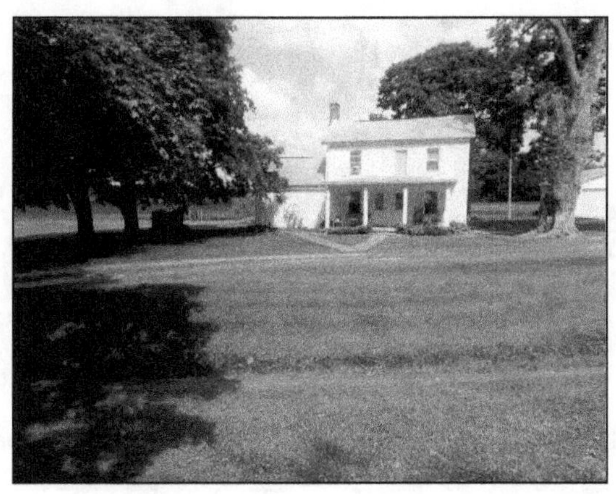

We looked at and eventually bought an old farmhouse and several adjoining acres. It was a nice old place. It needed some cleaning up and I refreshed the interior a little bit with some paint and a little handy-work. My dad and I even bought some cattle and put them out on our pasture.

Everything was going good. I started noticing that my wife was acting weird. She didn't seem very happy with me most of the time, but I wasn't exactly sure why. Well, I was working and making money, but I was still drinking a lot.

The Blizzard of '77

As winter approached, it was a colder than usual winter. I was working in Frankfort, Indiana. We had worked all week without stopping to go home. I was just finishing up on a Friday when it started to snow. At first a little, then it just dumped what seemed like tons of snow on us. We checked out of our motel rooms and headed home. We were just outside of town and found that the state police had the roads blocked. We were told to turn around.

"Fellas, there are people stranded. It's a blizzard and all the roads are impassable."

We headed back to the old motel. Our rooms were already rented out, but there were so many people stranded that we ended up staying in a one bedroom motel room for the night. There was the four of us and two guys we didn't even know. There were people sleeping in the lobby, in the office, anywhere they could. There were stranded people everywhere.

One of the guys with us had a four wheel drive truck and since we had been in the motel all week none of us had any money. We started driving around pulling people out of snow drifts and we made a couple of hundred dollars in about three hours. The weather had gotten so bad that we almost couldn't get back to the motel, so we decided we were done. The

Blizzard of 77 was what they called it. It was one of the worst on record. We stayed two weeks in that motel, mostly sleeping on the floor.

The National Guard started flying food and supplies into the town. When we finally did get out, I had been cold for so long that I stopped, picked up my check, cashed it and headed straight home. I didn't even pack my clothes, I just threw them in the back of the car. I needed a break. I took my wife and little girl and we went to Florida for a month. I was over Indiana weather.

After our vacation, we headed back home to the farmhouse. Things seemed to be going along pretty smooth. One day, I came home to find my wife sitting in the middle of our floor. She was inside a circle of lit candles on the living room floor of the old farmhouse, chanting. The baby was crying in her crib and she had completely ignored her.

"What are you doing?"

She almost growled at me and in a strange voice and said, "None of your business."

I felt this strange feeling, an uncomfortable feeling. I wasn't sure what it was that she was doing, but it was not good. I went on for about three months doing the same things; working, drinking, etc. I assumed everything was ok.

I later discovered that the old house where we lived had

been built originally in the 1700's. The Indians had attacked and killed the woman and some of her children there. They burnt the original log home to the ground. The man of the house had been gone and when he found them he buried his family and went back East. A few years later he had come back and rebuilt the home.

The old woman that we bought the house from had lived in it for several years, but her husband had gone mad while they lived there. One day, she came home and he had covered the whole yard in gravel. After he died, she sold it to her niece and her husband. They had some marital problems while living in that house. Supposedly, she turned really wild. She had even tried to come on to me when I met her.

I confronted my wife with her actions and told her I didn't want her burning the candles and chanting like that.

"I am going to follow MY god!" she said in quite a loud manner.

"What god are you talking about?" I asked.

"I am worshiping a god of Wicca."

I had no idea what that was, but I knew it wasn't good.

We didn't talk anymore about it for the rest of the weekend and I left for work in north central Indiana the following Monday morning. It was far enough away that I stayed all week and came home that Friday evening. When I got home, there was no one home. My wife and the baby were gone. I quickly made something to eat and grabbed a beer from the fridge sat down and turned on the TV. I wasn't sure where they were.

I heard the phone ring.

She said in an almost happy voice, "I have taken the baby and we aren't coming back."

I looked through the house and sure enough, their clothes were gone and she had taken all the cash we had saved back. I wasn't too worried. I figured she would be back, so I went to bed.

The next day, I went into town to get some cash out of the bank. On my way, I got stuck in a snow drift and ice tore a hole in my oil filter. I patched it up the best I could and eased the car into town. I stopped at the bank and they informed me that all of my accounts had been closed. My checking and savings were closed and there was no money. She had taken it all. Not only was the money all gone, but they informed me that the loans were all three months delinquent. She hadn't been paying our bills.

My wife had been planning for months and had taken all the money I made and her checks and kept it. No bills were getting paid. I had twelve dollars in my pocket and had a bad oil filter. I limped the car over to a gas station and asked the guy how much he charged for an oil change. He said fifteen dollars. I told him what happened and he agreed to take the twelve dollars I had and let me pay him the rest when I could.

I was devastated! I started drinking heavier than I had previously and was doing more and more drugs. Only now, it wasn't just pot once in a while. Before I knew it, my world had crashed around me. I was getting into arguments at work. Even with Grif. I had it out with the boss. I left that job and went to work in construction again. It was a way for me to earn a lot of money without having to be so mentally sharp. I just couldn't focus.

I was running around with guys from the more influential families in the area and now I was chasing women. Before I knew it, my downward spiral just hit bottom. I had lost everything. I had lost my family, the home I had worked so hard to get, and I was living with friends. I thought I had hit bottom!

Studying the Rich Folk

I began to think back to my dream of being rich. I decided that I needed to study rich people to see how they made their money and how they kept that money. I started my research of the rich and the first thing I found was there were three categories of the wealthy.

1. There were the people who inherited their wealth.

2. There were the people who 'Lucked' into large sums of money by winning the lottery, obtained it illegally by dealing drugs, or some other method of quick money. They never seemed to be able keep it. They always ended up losing it all.

3. Finally, there were those rich people who earned their money and kept it.

I knew the first category wasn't going to work for me, because, I knew I had no rich family who would leave me any money. The second category was either a stroke of luck or illegal and dangerous. I wasn't very lucky and I wanted to avoid jail. The third category was the only one that would work for me. After all, I was a hard worker, so if I found the right job or way to make money, then maybe I could do that. Even though I had worked hard and had money how could I learn to keep it.

As I continued my research on that category of people, I

found that a large percentage of those who earned and kept their wealth were Christians. I had always believed that God existed, after all, He had even spoken to me in the hay field when I was a kid. I really didn't know a lot about Him, other than the things my grandpa had taught me. I had never read the Bible, nor had I ever gone to church.

But, I decided if these people could get lots of money and live great lives, why not try God and see what would happen! So, I knelt down in my bedroom and prayed this prayer.

I said, **"God, if you will get me an excellent job where I can make lots of money and be able to have all these nice things, I will serve you. AMEN"**

That was it. Just a simple prayer from someone who didn't know how to pray.

Within a week I landed a new job. The job was estimating construction projects and selling the new construction or selling remodeling jobs. The first two days I earned $1,380. It was great, it was easy, and I enjoyed it. Life just kept getting better and better. I was making more money than I ever had in my entire life.

Life was great, except I was still living it up. I was drinking the best whiskey, driving nice cars, doing more drugs, dating a playboy playmate and other beautiful women. Life was good! Then the stroke of luck I was looking for. I sold a four-hundred house housing project. The potential income for me was well into the millions. I had **Arrived!** I was living in a beautiful beach house in Florida. I had it all. The only thing I wasn't doing right was serving God as I had promised.

Then, the economy took a big hit. People couldn't get financing for new homes. They couldn't even get gas for their automobiles.   There were gas lines at every gas station, everywhere. Before I knew it, I had lost it all.   Even my influential friends disappeared once the money ran out. I couldn't get a job and I ended up without a place to stay. I had no money for rent and the landlord said I would have to get out. I was half-starved, exhausted and had just absolutely hit rock bottom. I was so far down I had to look up to see the bottom.

I was living on the riverbank, so I started eating whatever fish I could catch. One day, even the river dried up, it seemed, and I couldn't even catch fish. This went on for days.

I bought a junk car from my brother on payments. Imagine going from all kinds of money to a point where I'm making payments on a one-hundred-fifty dollar car. I found myself living on a riverbank, out in the country. My uncle finally felt sorry for me and gave me a job. I was making a hundred dollars a week, before taxes. I slept wherever I could. I was able to get a second job working part-time in the evenings.

I found an old house for rent. It was a hundred dollars a month and they let me make payments on the first month's rent. I moved in, but I had no furniture. I remember sleeping on a dirty, muddy sleeping bag that first night. When I woke up, I had sun light shining in my eyes and it wasn't from a window. It was beaming in through a crack in the wall. I opened my eyes to look around and I could see other cracks letting light shine through.

There I was starting with nothing all over again. Only this time, I had no friends. My family didn't even want me around. I was a mess and I couldn't blame them. It was just me. Oh, but, I still managed to get beer and occasionally a drink. I still had a few people who were willing to share a joint with me.

I was working 16 hours a day for less than two-hundred dollars a week. By the time I bought cigarettes, beer and gasoline, pretty much I was broke again, but I felt I was on the comeback trail.

One day, I got called into the office at work. They laid me off. *OK, fine,* I thought. *I still have the evening job at least I could have some money.* When I went to work that same evening, they said they couldn't use me anymore. Once again, I had no work, no money. I spent the next two weeks looking for work. I had found nothing and had completely run out of money. No food, I was starving and no prospect for a job.

I sat at home and had managed to find four beers alongside of the road. I drank 4 beers. I drank those and then drank a bottle of vodka I had saved for the worst days. I picked up an old double barrel shotgun I had been given, loaded it and went outside.

I sat down on an old picnic table and said, "I'm done with this life. I can't take it anymore I have tried everything. I have tried everything." I cursed God I said, "Why make me suffer like this."

The old gun had dual hammers and as I cocked the hammers on the shotgun, some local guys were working nearby and I heard one say, "Hey, what is that guy doing over there?" He was pointing at me. "He looks like he's going to kill himself."

Another guy said, "Oh that's just Stanton. Let him, it's no loss."

You would think after hearing that, I would come to my senses, but I was still determined to end it all. I put the shotgun under my chin, kicked my shoe off my right foot and put my big toe on the dual triggers. Just as I was going to push the triggers down, God called to me. He said in an audible voice, not in my heart or my head. I actually heard Him speak.

I heard him say, **"Raymond, you haven't tried me yet."**

I quickly said, "Yes, I did. I prayed and you gave me the job."

He said**, "No, you said you would serve me and you didn't serve me. You haven't tried me. Try me and see that I am good."**

There was no doubt in my mind that it was God. I figured everyone around could hear Him because it was so loud and clear.

"Ok, God. You take my life, I'm done with it. I am not going to help you. I am not going to do anything. You take my life and do what you will with it," I said.

I took my toe off the triggers. I still don't know how the gun didn't go off. I took it out from under my chin, let the hammers off and went into the house. I threw the gun down and sat down in an old chair. I wept for the first time in years.

I sat there for a while to see what would happen. I was waiting. *What would God do now?* Nothing, He did nothing. I got up and turned on a little 12-inch black and white TV that I had taken out of a dumpster. It barely worked, but I got 3 regular channels and three uhf channels. It took some time to warm up, but once it did, the evangelist, Jimmy Swaggart was on. I heard him say, 'You there in your living room, kneel down right there and accept Christ'.

I turned the channel. The second channel also had Jimmy Swaggart on it. Once again, he said, 'You, right there in your living room, kneel down and accept Jesus'.

I turned the channel once more and there he was again. I switched to the uhf channels. Every channel I turned to, Jimmy Swaggart was on. I stopped on the last channel and he said, 'You, right there in your living room. God just spoke to you. He just kept you from taking your own life. Kneel down and accept Christ now, this is your time'.

I immediately knelt down right there in that old dirty house and repeated the prayer he had spoken to me to say. I accepted Jesus that day.

It was like the whole world lifted off my shoulders; everything just melted away and I fell asleep. All night long I had visions of different things, one after the other God would show me things.

I was exhausted but refreshed when I awoke the next morning. My grandfather came and asked me to come to his house for breakfast. He said he had some roof work he needed me to do for him. I finished what he needed done and as he was paying me, one of my uncles came over.

"Hey, Raymond, someone called for you. He wants you

to start work immediately."

I Was Changed!

My life changed from that day on. I never went back to the drinking or the drugs.

Let me tell you what God did for me. He restored unto me my family. He restored unto me a home. He restored unto me my finances. Most importantly, He restored unto me a new heart. What do I mean by this? He changed me completely. He gave me a life of joy, peace and hope. He gave me a new life.

I have been following Him ever since that day. I can tell you **that what He has done for me, He can do for you.** While He may not speak to you audibly, as He did to me, He has directed me to write this so you can read it and know He is there for you. He is there no matter what you have done. He is there no matter how you have failed. He loves you and wants to minister to you.

I have told my story to thousands around the world and they have accepted Christ as their savior.

It is true, as you now know, because I believe you can feel

the truth in it. I am sure it must have touched your heart. Will you kneel down, now? Kneel down right where you are and accept Jesus. Just say this prayer and believe it and you will see that God is so good. Try Him and you will see.

Say this prayer: ***Dear God, I know that I have failed at life. I have sinned and done wrong. I ask that You forgive me and take over my life. You know that I can't live it by myself, I need your help. I accept You as my Lord and Savior. In the name of Jesus I ask it, Amen.***

I don't know how you feel after saying that prayer, but I can tell you when I said that prayer all those years ago, it was as if a huge weight was lifted from me. It was like the whole world was taken off my shoulders. For the first time in years, I felt clean inside. It was as if a peace settled over my life. It was the peace of God. Do you feel it?

You see, I have written this book to show you the truth. The truth is that God wants a relationship with you and by accepting Him as God over your life, you have started a closer relationship with Him.

The way to have any relationship is to talk to one another. Without communication a relationship will not grow. God wants you to communicate with Him, so pray and talk with Him often.

The best way is to just talk to Him like He is your Father,

which He is. He is your Spiritual Father. Ask Him what He wants from you. Tell Him your heart's desire and always end by saying, *In Jesus' name I ask.*

John 14:12-14 *12 Verily, verily, I say unto you, he that believeth on me, the works that I do shall he do also; and greater (works) than these shall he do; because I go unto the Father.13 And whatsoever ye shall ask in my name, that will I do, that the Father may be glorified in the Son.14 If ye shall ask anything in my name, that will I do. 4. Jesus is the way to the Father God. John 14:6 Jesus saith unto him, I am the way, the truth, and the life: no man cometh unto the Father, but by me.*

Now to answer a couple of questions that you will most certainly have. These will be the truth, no preachy stuff.

First, you are now a Christian. You have just begun a new life. In the Church world you will hear it called being *Born Again* or being *Saved.* The reason it is called being *Born Again,* is that you have just started a new life. A life without all the sins of your old existence. You have been saved from the spiritual death of sin. All the wrongs or sins you have done in your past are forgiven at this very moment by God and will be remembered against you no more.

One of the questions that I am asked often when I offer counseling is: *"I still remember the things I have done in the past. I'm not sure that I'm forgiven."*

God is not a man that He should lie. Your sins are forgiven just as His word says. Satan will try to remind you of them, to make you feel guilty. But, if God has forgiven you, who is Satan to bring it up to you? As for you, if God has forgiven you, who are you to not forgive yourself?

Psalms 103:11-13 *11 For as high as the heavens are above the earth, so great is his love for those who fear him; 12 as far as the east is from the west, so far has removed our transgressions from us. 13 As a father has compassion on his children, so the LORD has compassion on those who fear him;*

Second, you are saved. The next question I am asked is, "Do I have to go to church to be saved?" No, you don't have to go to church to be saved. That happened the minute you finished the prayer and meant it. But, you should pray for the Lord to direct you to the right church for you. You should try to attend regularly, because it will help you grow spiritually and help give you strength in your new walk following Christ.

John 8:31-32 *31 To those who had believed him, Jesus said, 'If you hold to my teaching, you are really my disciples. 32 Then you will know the truth, and the truth will set you free'.*

The things that I have written in this pamphlet are true and I have found that the one constant truth is the Lord Jesus. As the scripture above says, He is the way the truth and the life. My prayer for you is that this has touched your life in a very positive way and that you have started that new relationship with the Heavenly Father and His son the Lord Jesus.

My Truth is not over yet, evidently God is not done with me. The visions God shared with me have been coming to pass. I see them being fulfilled by me, through God using me, and through others. I am currently working on my second book. I will write more about the visions I have experienced in the next book.

 **Author Pastor Ray Stanton** felt the calling from God most of his life, but it wasn't until he was twenty-seven years old, at the lowest point that he discovered God's love.

Ray is a graduate of Baptist Seminary and holds a Master's degree. He has been a pastor for over thirty years. Pastor Ray recently started What God Wants Ministries with his wife, Debi.

He has traveled to Israel, Jordan and all over the United States spreading God's love. He has made several mission trips to Honduras where he works with Pastor Carlos Caceres of Prince of Peace Church. What God Wants Ministries helps to support the little church of less than thirty members.

I would love to hear from you and hear about your experience.

You can contact me at raymark_99@yahoo.com.

It is Pastor Stanton's wish for you that this book be an inspiration in your walk with God. It is his hope that you will experience the love of God and continue to grow in your relationship with God.

God Bless and Keep You!